NEW
GERMAN
COOKING

Recipes for Classics Revisited

NEW GERMAN COOKING

JEREMY & JESSICA NOLEN

with **DREW LAZOR**
photographs by **JASON VARNEY**

CHRONICLE BOOKS

SAN FRANCISCO

Library of Congress Cataloging-in-Publication Data available
ISBN 978-1-4521-2806-1

Manufactured in China

Design by The Heads of State
Prop and food styling by Carrie Purcell

10 9 8 7 6 5 4 3 2 1

Chronicle Books LLC
680 Second Street
San Francisco, California 94107
www.chroniclebooks.com

CONTENTS

INTRODUCTION

SAUSAGE, SCHNITZEL, SAUERKRAUT.

ASK MOST PEOPLE what comes to mind when they hear the phrase *German food* and the response is likely to be those three dishes, quickly followed by such adjectives as *heavy, fatty*, and *meat obsessed*. Germany is thought of as a nation of mirthful drinkers, their food nothing more than the fuel that soaks up the beer. In other words, the German kitchen is regarded as hearty and serviceable but certainly not great.

Here in the United States, German cuisine is never discussed with the same reverence accorded the tables of France, Italy, and Spain. This is, of course, nonsense. For far too long, German cooking has been underrated outside of its national boundaries, and this book aims to change that. *New German Cooking* celebrates the flavor, freshness, variety, and seasonality of German cuisine.

The earliest German immigrants to the United States, who began arriving in the late 1600s from the west-central region known today as the Rhineland-Palatine, established themselves as farmers in the Midwest and the Mid-Atlantic. By the mid-nineteenth century, the period that saw the heaviest influx of German immigrants up to that point, major cities like New York, Philadelphia, and Saint Louis had developed thriving German populations of their own.

During this period, many of the German restaurants opened by immigrants in metropolitan areas, such as Boston's Jacob Wirth or The Berghoff in Chicago (both still in business), built their menus around food native to the mountains of Bavaria. Over time, dishes like pretzels, *Weisswurst,* potato salad, and sauerbraten grew to define German food in America, even though they represented only a fraction of the tradition. Bavarian social culture, with its oompah bands and giant beer steins, became synonymous with German culture, as well.

Just like France, Italy, or Spain, Germany is a country of regional cuisines representing a staggering diversity of dishes, styles, and ingredients. In the north, along the border with Denmark, seafood pulled from the Baltic Sea and the North Atlantic dominates cutting boards. French influences creep into

the cooking around the Black Forest area, bordered on the west by Alsace-Lorraine. The west-central region of Westphalia is widely known for the acorn-fed hogs used for making the area's famous juniper-cured hams, a centuries-old practice that yields a product reminiscent of the *jamón ibérico* of Spain. To the east, where Germany borders the Czech Republic and Poland, Slavic influences like dumplings and stuffed cabbage define everyday cooking. Even major cities like Munich and Frankfurt have dining traditions that are underexposed outside the country's borders.

Germany's culinary wealth, bolstered by a strong agricultural backbone, seasonal appeal, and methods that span generations, suggest that it's a nation ripe for international recognition—and it is starting to roll in. As of 2012, the country features the third highest number of Michelin-starred restaurants on the planet, after France and Italy. But the cuisine continues to struggle to find a foothold in America, which has never been known for high-quality German restaurants and chefs. How can we start to truly appreciate German food in the United States? The answer to that begins with Jeremy's story.

FROM READING TO PHILADELPHIA

Jeremy's unconventional journey into German cooking

I was born in California, but my family relocated near to Reading, Pennsylvania, when I was four years old. If I had stayed on the West Coast, I could very well have ended up handling more serrano chiles than spaetzle. But growing up in the heart of Pennsylvania Dutch country established my fascination with German food early. My father, Ron, has been a chef all my

life, and some of my best childhood memories include visiting the butchers at Reading's Fairgrounds Farmers Market every Saturday to purchase sausages and liverwurst for weekend family dinners.

Germans first came to Pennsylvania in 1683, making it home to the longest-established German American population in the country. For both recent immigrants and those looking to stay in touch with their German heritage, my hometown features two private organizations, the Reading Liederkranz and the Evergreen Country Club. Both sponsor fund-raisers, dance lessons, and soccer leagues and take food and drink very seriously, hosting an elaborate annual Oktoberfest. (The Liederkranz's Oktoberfest, which draws thousands of revelers every year over its four-day run, is the oldest celebration of its kind in the state.) When I was a teenager, my father took a weekend consultancy at the Evergreen, in addition to his regular chef job, and he brought me in to help him out. Our cooking eventually caught the attention of the Liederkranz folks, and they lured me away from the Evergreen—and away from my dad—to run their restaurant.

It was at the Liederkranz that I really began to learn about German food, absorbing everything I could from the team of elderly German cooks looking to cede control of the kitchen to a younger generation. It began with the basics, like German potato salad: simply potatoes boiled in their skins, plus onions, vinegar, and parsley, served at room temperature. No mayo and definitely no bacon, even though much of America seems to think you need those things to make the salad German. Satisfied with my sauerbraten and *Rouladen,* I eventually gained the confidence to begin experimenting. I would go to the farmers' market and buy the produce and meats that looked best, using them to create nontraditional dishes that were German in spirit. Duck and fish, neither of which have much of a place in German American cooking, began showing up on my menu. More unfamiliar techniques and ingredients I'd studied on my own found their way onto my everyday prep lists, too.

Eventually I left Liederkranz and worked in a variety of different restaurant kitchens before finally landing in Philadelphia in 2006, where I continued to find restaurant work. None of the kitchens was German, but I found ways to sneak my version of German dishes onto specials boards. It was at Coquette, a neighborhood French bistro where I served as head chef, that people began to notice my German-inspired dishes on the menu. (This is also where I met my wife, Jessica, who is in charge of all things sweet in the world of new German cooking.) A regular customer who liked my Alsatian-inspired plates introduced me to Doug and Kelly Hager, who opened Brauhaus Schmitz, with me in the kitchen, in 2009.

A REAL GERMAN BIERHALLE

Located on Philadelphia's historic South Street, Brauhaus Schmitz is a true German beer hall, complete with perky servers decked out in traditional garb and the best teams of Bundesliga, Germany's premier soccer league, battling their way to victory across flat-screen TVs in the dining room. The draft lines of the two bars, in the lively dual-level front room and in the adjoining Brauer Bund (Brewer's Guild), are regularly connected to kegs that are either scarce or unavailable in the rest of the country. (Doug believes it is the finest German draft selection in the United States.) Both the staff and the crowds love to have fun—we are stocked with plenty of *Bierstiefeln*, giant boot-shaped beer

steins, and a shot ski for group schnapps sessions—but we've worked hard over the years to make sure our guests know us as more than just a party place. Toward that end, a sizable portion of the menu consists of familiar German American classics executed at a high level.

Early on, once we had nailed down all of the tried-and-true standards—sauerbraten, *Jägerschnitzel*, Nuremberg-style bratwurst doled out by the meter—we decided that Wednesday, a.k.a. Fun Day, would be the day we created new dishes. Perhaps we would focus on a homemade sausage for a special *Schlachtplatte* (a traditional plate of mixed meats and sausages), such as a precise combination of duck and pork meat and fat blended with a pungent smoked barley malt acquired from Aecht Schlenkerla, Germany's premier brewer of *Rauchbier* (smoked beer). Or we might experiment with cold smoking duck breasts cured in black pepper, juniper, and bay leaves for a new take on Westphalian ham. One day, we pounded sweetbreads, fried them to resemble schnitzel, and then dressed them up neo-Holsteiner style, with a caper-anchovy-egg sauce. On another Wednesday, we married a flat-iron pork steak, a cut not served anywhere in Germany, to smoked potatoes, a hearty corn-parsnip-leek hash, and a pretty parsley purée. To surprise diners who believe that German food is all about meat, we stuffed the traditionally meat-filled pasta known as *Maultaschen* with a spinach-and-potato mixture and topped it with an elegant chanterelle sauce and crumbled goat cheese.

Jessica, in her very important role as Brauhaus Schmitz's pastry chef and head baker, has embraced the new German approach, too, mixing in reimagined cookies, cakes, and desserts with her more traditional workload of

breads and pastries. This spirit of experimentation, coupled with a respect for and fascination with all aspects of German cuisine that are underexposed in America, is at the heart of new German cooking.

ABOUT THE RECIPES

As chefs, we are proud of what we have accomplished at Brauhaus Schmitz, but it is important to point out that this book is *not* a collection of restaurant-style recipes. The dishes, both sweet and savory, you will find here are designed to be prepared by home cooks and served family-style.

The recipes do vary in level of difficulty, however. Some processes, such as sausage making, sauerkraut fermentation, and meat smoking, call for a heightened attention to detail and greater familiarity with less-common techniques. Others, like our Grilled Marinated Chicken with Paprika (page 98), Spicy Marinated Pork Skewers with Peppers, Onions, and Zucchini (page 132), and Grilled Salmon with Horseradish and Pickled Beet Sauce (page 87), are easy-to-prepare fare for a weeknight dinner. Some dishes, like *Hasenpfeffer* (see page 140) and Christmas goose (see page 105), are beloved classics, while others, like Foie Gras Liverwurst (page 112) and Truffled Hazelnut and Potato Soup (page 73), are more imaginative by design, a reflection of our Fun Day explorations. Regardless of which recipes you choose, our aim is to provide you with big, boldly seasoned, inspiring, honest dishes that we hope you'll be proud to serve to your family and friends.

In many ways, our entire cooking careers to this point have led us to this book, which we have been thrilled to put together. The many hours we have spent recipe testing, researching, and traveling have been an investment in a simple goal: exposing as many people as possible to the state of modern German cuisine, which is so much more diverse than most observers realize. For us, the key word is *balance,* whether we are discussing ingredients, execution, or the vital role that the past plays in the present.

But some traditions never change regardless of what the calendar says. Whether we are placing a spotlight on lesser-known aspects of German cuisine unfamiliar to the American palate, introducing our own ideas, or marrying these two approaches, our take on new German cooking is at its best when it is shared.

1

BREADS & SPREADS

BROTZEIT

BROTZEIT LITERALLY MEANS "BREAD TIME," but there's much more to this German tradition than a few buddies splitting a loaf of pumpernickel. Similar in spirit to tapas in Spain, antipasti in Italy, or even afternoon tea in England, Brotzeit describes the array of hot and cold spreads, cheeses, meats, open-face sandwiches, and other snacks served for a party or a casual get-together.

Pay a social visit to a German home and it's likely a Brotzeit spread will appear right after you say your hellos, especially if you arrive in the afternoon lull between lunch and dinner. It's typically simple. For example, at a friend's guesthouse in Bavaria, we were greeted with bread, butter, cheese, a few different types of salami, and a ramekin of *Griebenschmalz*, a buttery spread of pork fat mixed with crunchy cracklings. When we stopped by the Ayinger Brewery near Munich, owner Franz Inselkammer treated us to boards of pretzels, rye, cured meats, and pickles, accompanied, of course, with beer.

When Jeremy was growing up, his parents would put together their own Brotzeit spreads for company, whether it was a small gathering of family members or a spirited New Year's Eve party. This chapter mixes German entertaining traditions with what Jeremy recalls from those early days. The dishes are easy to prepare and easy to eat, which keeps the focus where it should be: on friends and family.

BAVARIAN PRETZELS
LAUGENBREZEL

OUR AT-HOME QUEST to make the perfect Bavarian *Laugenbrezel*, or soft pretzel, which took place long before Brauhaus Schmitz opened, stretched out over the course of a year. Every Sunday, we would experiment with different recipes, never quite nailing the unmistakable balance—crusty outside, soft inside, both sweet and salty—that we desired. Finally, after dozens of stutter starts, we nailed it. Combining bread flour and all-purpose flour helped achieve the correct texture, while a traditional lye dip (wear gloves and don't worry, as it won't be like when Tyler burned Jack's hands with the stuff in *Fight Club*), helped with that elusive pretzel chew. We love them at the restaurant, and it seems others agree—in 2010, this pretzel won Best of Philly in *Philadelphia* magazine, and we serve about fifteen thousand of them a year.

You can shape these pretzels in a variety of ways, such as long sticks, rolls, or the traditional crossed-armed, or symmetrical looped form, which is described here. Serve the pretzels plain or with butter, whole-grain mustard, cheeses, and/or cold meats, and, of course, with a good lager.

NOTE: *We weigh all of the ingredients in this recipe in grams (except for the water for the lye dip), due to the precision necessary in baking. For the best results, use a digital scale.*

INGREDIENTS (MAKES 4 TO 6 PRETZELS)

235 g room-temperature water	130 g bread flour	**LYE DIP**
5 g sugar	430 g all-purpose flour, plus more for dusting	15 g food-grade lye
35 g unsalted butter	5 g kosher salt	2 cups/480 ml cold water
55 g buttermilk	Nonstick cooking spray for preparing the pan	Everything Pretzel Topping (recipe follows; optional)
30 g fresh yeast		Kosher salt (optional)

1. In a stand mixer fitted with the dough hook, combine the room-temperature water, sugar, butter, and buttermilk, then crumble in the yeast. Mix on low speed until the yeast has dissolved. The butter will still be chunky. Add the bread flour and all-purpose flour and continue to mix on low speed until the dough starts to come together in a shaggy mass, about 1 minute. Add the salt, increase the mixer speed to medium, and knead the dough until it looks dense and is moist and smooth, 5 to 7 minutes.

2. Cut the dough into four to six equal portions. Lightly dust a work surface with all-purpose flour and put one portion of the dough on the floured surface. Using your palms in a back-and-forth motion, roll the dough into a rope about 24 in/ 61 cm long and ¾ in/2 cm thick. Keeping the center of the rope on the work surface, pick up one end with each hand and cross one end over the other to form a loose loop, then twist the ends around each other once. Now, fold the twisted ends over the opposite end of the loop, then attach one end to each side of the loop. If desired, using the tip of a paring knife, make a slash about 2 in/5 cm long and ½ in/12 mm deep along the bottom edge of the pretzel, to give it an authentic look. Repeat with the remaining dough portions.

3. Preheat the oven to 375°F/190°C. Line a large sheet pan with parchment paper and coat the paper with nonstick cooking spray.

4. *To make the lye dip,* in a medium bowl, combine the lye and cold water and stir to dissolve the lye.

5. One at a time, fully submerge the pretzels in the lye solution, then transfer them to the prepared sheet pan. Let the pretzels rise until they are almost doubled in volume, 10 to 15 minutes.

6. Sprinkle the pretzels generously with topping (if using); otherwise sprinkle with salt. Bake the pretzels, rotating the pan back to front at the halfway point to ensure even baking, until the tops are evenly dark golden brown, 10 to 15 minutes. Let the pretzels cool on the pan for at least 10 minutes before serving. The pretzels taste best the day they are baked. Any leftovers can be saved for making croutons.

EVERYTHING PRETZEL TOPPING

INGREDIENTS (MAKES ENOUGH FOR 4 TO 6 PRETZELS)

1 tbsp dried onion flakes

1 tbsp dried garlic flakes (not granulated or powder)

½ tsp anise seed

1 tsp dill seeds

½ tsp black pepper

1 tbsp poppy seeds

1 tbsp sesame seeds

1 tbsp coarse salt

In a spice grinder, combine the onion flakes, garlic flakes, anise seed, dill seeds, and pepper and pulse until coarsely ground. Pour into a small bowl and stir in the poppy seeds, sesame seeds, and salt.

SOURDOUGH BARLEY BREAD
WITH SAGE TOPPING
GERSTENBROT

THE IDEA BEHIND THIS RECIPE was to produce something both nostalgic and slightly unfamiliar—in other words, something truly new German in approach. Grains, seeds, and nuts are used in many everyday German breads, which is why barley, given its essential role in brewing, seemed like a logical inclusion. Before baking, we slather these hand-formed loaves with a paste of sage, salt, and olive oil, which bakes into a thick crust—that's the "unfamiliar" part. Be gentle with the dough; it is folded, never truly kneaded. Its hearty characteristics can contribute to a dense final product if overworked.

You will need a sourdough starter to make this bread. If you don't have one on hand, use the White Sourdough Starter (which, despite the name, is actually a preferment, rather than a starter) on page 24 or purchase or otherwise acquire a starter of your own. This bread itself is extremely versatile. It can be served with any of the dishes in this chapter or used for toast or sandwiches.

NOTE: *We weigh all of the ingredients in this recipe in grams (except the topping ingredients and the water for baking), due to the precision necessary in baking. For the best results, use a digital scale.*

INGREDIENTS (MAKES 2 MEDIUM-SIZE LOAVES)

SPONGE

90 g medium rye flour

15 g active dry yeast

1 g kosher salt

120 g warm water
(100°F/38°C)

200 g pearl barley

655 g water

225 g sourdough starter

15 g fresh yeast

20 g sugar

20 g kosher salt

Nonstick cooking spray
for preparing the pan

TOPPING

½ cup/120 ml olive oil

1 tbsp kosher salt

2 tbsp finely chopped
fresh sage leaves

1 cup/240 ml water

1. *To make the sponge,* in a medium bowl, combine the rye flour, active dry yeast, salt, and warm water and stir until the flour is evenly moistened. Cover loosely with a kitchen towel and let stand in a warm place for 2 hours.

2. Preheat the oven to 375°F/190°C.

3. Spread the barley on a rimmed sheet pan and toast in the oven until golden brown, about 15 minutes. Transfer the barley to a medium saucepan, add 470 g of the water, cover, and bring to a boil over high heat. Lower the heat to a simmer and cook until almost all of the water is absorbed, about 30 minutes. Pour the cooked barley onto a sheet pan and let cool completely.

4. In a large bowl, combine the sponge, sourdough starter, cooked barley, the remaining 185 g water, the fresh yeast, sugar, and salt and mix with a wooden spoon until a soft ball of dough forms. Cover the bowl with plastic wrap and let the dough rest in a warm area (about 80°F/27°C) for 1½ hours. Every 30 minutes, "fold" the dough once: stretch the four corners out and then rejoin them in the middle.

5. Coat a half sheet pan with cooking spray. Remove the dough from the bowl, divide it in half, and shape each half into a round loaf. Place the loaves on the prepared sheet pan, spacing them at least 4 in/10 cm apart, cover loosely with a clean kitchen towel, and refrigerate overnight.

6. The next day, place a metal container, such as a baking pan, on the lower rack in the oven and preheat the oven to 450°F/230°C.

7. *To make the topping,* in a small bowl, stir together the olive oil, salt, and sage, mixing well.

8. Divide the sage mixture in half and spread evenly over the top of each loaf. Place the sheet pan with the loaves on the middle rack of the oven, pour the 1 cup/240 ml water into the preheated container on the lower rack, and quickly close the oven door. Bake for 15 minutes, then lower the heat to 400°F/200°C and continue to bake until the loaves are dark golden brown and emit a hollow sound when tapped on the bottom, about 10 minutes longer.

9. Transfer the loaves to a wire rack and let cool for at least 1 hour before serving. Wrap any leftover bread in plastic wrap and store at room temperature for up to 3 days.

WHITE SOURDOUGH STARTER

THIS RECIPE is more of a simple preferment, ready in one or two days, than a starter, which is traditionally made by alternately discarding a portion of the water-flour mixture and feeding it with more water and flour over the course of several days. You will end up with more than you need for the barley bread on page 22 and just the amount you need for the flaxseed bread on the facing page. Any excess can be discarded.

INGREDIENTS (MAKES ABOUT 540 G)

2 cups/480 ml water

2 cups/280 g bread flour

In a glass bowl or other nonreactive container, stir together the water and flour until well mixed. Cover loosely with a clean kitchen towel and let stand at warm room temperature for 24 hours. At this point, check the mixture to see if bubbles have begun to form. If they have, and the mixture smells sour, it is ready to use. If it does not smell sour, leave it out at room temperature for another 24 hours, then use.

GOLDEN FLAXSEED MIXED BREAD

LEINSAMEN MISCHBROT

MISCHBROT **MEANS "MIXED BREAD"** and refers to the use of multiple flours to create a desired flavor and texture profile. Our Mischbrot uses spelt, rye, oat, and wheat flours, plus golden flaxseeds. It is a good choice for health-conscious people who still want to enjoy bread, because the flour blend provides an abundance of vitamins, minerals, fiber, proteins, and complex carbohydrates. If we were asked to recommend a "daily bread" to eat with just about everything, this would be it. You can use it for toast and sandwiches and for topping with spreads and cured meats.

NOTE: *We weigh all of the ingredients in this recipe in grams (except for the water for baking), due to the precision necessary in baking. For the best results, use a digital scale.*

INGREDIENTS (MAKES 2 MEDIUM-SIZE LOAVES)

MASH

480 g whole milk

5 g sugar

5 g salt

100 g oat flour

540 g White Sourdough Starter (facing page)

100 g spelt flour

510 g bread flour

90 g medium rye flour

17 g kosher salt

20 g fresh yeast

30 g golden flaxseeds

40 g malt powder

235 g water

Canola oil for oiling the bowl

Nonstick cooking spray for preparing the pan

1 cup/240 ml water

1. *To make the mash,* in a small saucepan, combine the milk, sugar, and salt over high heat. Bring to a boil and remove from the heat. Pour in the oat flour and stir until the flour is evenly moistened. Let sit just until the milk is absorbed.

2. In a large bowl, combine the mash, sourdough starter, spelt flour, bread flour, rye flour, salt, yeast, flaxseeds, malt powder, and water and stir with a wooden spoon until mixed. Then, using your hands, knead the mixture in the bowl until a soft ball of dough forms.

3. Oil a large bowl. Transfer the ball of dough to the oiled bowl, turn the dough to coat with the oil, and cover the bowl with plastic wrap. Place the bowl in a warm area until the dough almost doubles in volume, about 1 hour.

4. Punch the dough down in the bowl and then fold it onto itself. Re-cover the bowl and let the dough rise again until it doubles in volume, about 30 minutes. Repeat punching down the dough, folding it, and letting it rise again two more times.

(Continued)

5. Coat a half sheet pan with cooking spray. Remove the dough from the bowl, divide it in half, and shape each half into a round loaf. Place the loaves on the prepared sheet, spacing them at least 4 in/10 cm apart, cover loosely with a clean kitchen towel, and refrigerate overnight.

6. The next day, place a metal container, such as a baking pan, on the lower rack in the oven and preheat the oven to 450°F/230°C.

7. Place the sheet pan with the loaves on the middle rack of the oven, pour the 1 cup/240 ml water into the heated container on the lower rack, and quickly close the oven door. Bake until the loaves are dark golden brown and emit a hollow sound when tapped on the bottom, about 30 minutes.

8. Transfer the loaves to a wire rack and let cool for at least 1 hour before serving. Wrap any leftover bread in plastic wrap and store at room temperature for up to 24 hours; then refrigerate for up to 1 week.

CRISPY SAUERKRAUT FRITTERS

SAUERKRAUT KROKETTEN

IF YOU KNOW PEOPLE who say they do not like sauerkraut, get them to try one of these fritters. Jeremy's parents always prepared these *Kroketten* for parties when Jeremy was a child. Smoked sausage, bacon, and kraut in a crunchy fried shell, dipped in a sweet-and-spicy mustard sauce—it is difficult to think of a better item for Brotzeit, especially if beer is involved. *Bauernwurst,* or "peasant's sausage," is a coarsely textured, richly seasoned smoked pork sausage that is commonly grilled and served in a bun or alongside salad or sauerkraut. These fritters also hold up well at room temperature, making them ideal for serving as hors d'oeuvres.

INGREDIENTS (SERVES 4 TO 6)

FILLING

4 slices thick-cut bacon, finely diced

1 Bauernwurst, kielbasa, or other smoked sausage, about 6 oz/170 g, finely diced

1 lb/455 g sauerkraut, homemade (see page 194) or store-bought, drained

1 cup/80 g panko bread crumbs

1 cup/105 g grated Emmentaler, Gruyère, or Swiss cheese

2 eggs, lightly beaten

2 tbsp Löwensenf or Dijon spicy mustard

1½ cups/210 g all-purpose flour

½ tsp salt

¼ tsp freshly ground black pepper

3 eggs

1½ cups/120 g panko bread crumbs

Canola oil for deep-frying

1 cup/240 ml mayonnaise

2 tbsp honey

½ cup/120 ml whole-grain mustard, homemade (see page 196) or store-bought

1. *To make the filling,* in a medium frying pan, cook the bacon and sausage over medium heat, stirring occasionally, until the bacon is crisp but not too dark and the sausage is lightly browned, about 5 minutes. Remove the pan from the heat and let the contents cool completely. Save the rendered fat that remains in the pan along with the meat (the fat will add flavor).

2. In a large bowl, combine the sauerkraut, bread crumbs, cheese, eggs, and mustard and mix well. Add the bacon, sausage, and rendered fat to the bowl and mix well. The mixture should be a little firm or the fritters will fall apart during cooking. (If it is too loose, mix in additional bread crumbs as needed to achieve a tight consistency.)

3. Have ready a large plate or sheet pan. In a medium bowl, stir together the flour, salt, and pepper. In a second medium bowl, beat the eggs until blended. Put the bread crumbs in a third medium bowl. Using your hands, shape the filling mixture into balls slightly larger than a golf ball and pass them, one at a time, through each bowl: dredge evenly in flour, shaking off the excess; coat with egg, allowing the excess to drip off; and, finally, coat with bread crumbs, again shaking off the excess. As each fritter is breaded, set it on the plate. When all of the fritters are coated, cover and refrigerate overnight. The colder the fritters are, the better they will fry.

4. The next day, pour the canola oil to a depth of 3 in/7.5 cm into a Dutch oven or small stockpot and heat to 350°F/180°C. (If you don't have a thermometer, drop a pinch of bread crumbs into the oil. If the crumbs sizzle immediately, the oil is ready.) Line a large plate with paper towels.

5. Working in small batches to avoiding crowding, carefully add the cold fritters, one at a time, to the hot oil and fry until golden brown, 5 to 6 minutes. Using a slotted spoon, transfer the fritters to the towel-lined plate to drain and place in a warm oven. Repeat with the remaining fritters.

6. While the fritters are frying, in a small bowl, stir together the mayonnaise, honey, and mustard, mixing well, to use as a dipping sauce.

7. Arrange the fritters on a platter and serve with the mustard.

GREEN ASPARAGUS AND AGED GOUDA DIP

SPARGELAUFSTRICH

THIS CROWD-PLEASER takes asparagus, one of Germany's most commonly prepared vegetables, and marries it with a pair of cheeses: cream cheese for the base, then salty, savory aged Gouda for flavor. We like to use Dutch-made Prima Donna, a cheese that marries the best qualities of Parmesan and Gruyère, in place of the standard Gouda. The dip can be served hot or at room temperature.

INGREDIENTS (SERVES 4 TO 6)

1 tbsp canola oil

1 tbsp unsalted butter

1 lb/455 g green asparagus, tough ends trimmed and spears cut crosswise into 1-in/2.5-cm pieces

4 shallots, sliced

4 garlic cloves, minced

½ cup/120 ml Riesling

Juice of 1 lemon

1 tsp finely chopped fresh thyme

1 tsp finely chopped fresh marjoram

1 tsp kosher salt

¼ tsp freshly ground black pepper

8 oz/225 g cream cheese, at room temperature

¼ cup/60 ml mayonnaise

3 oz/85 g aged Gouda or Prima Donna cheese, grated

Rye or sourdough bread for serving

1. In a medium frying pan, heat the canola oil and butter over medium-high heat. When hot, add the asparagus and cook, stirring occasionally, for 4 minutes. Add the shallots and garlic and cook and stir until the shallots and garlic are lightly browned, about 3 minutes longer. Pour in the Riesling and lemon juice and cook until the liquid is reduced by half, about 4 minutes. Add the thyme, marjoram, salt, and pepper and stir well. Remove the pan from the heat and transfer the mixture to a medium bowl.

2. Preheat the oven to 400°F/200°C. Have ready a 2-qt/2-L baking dish.

3. In a stand mixer fitted with the paddle attachment, combine the cream cheese, mayonnaise, and Gouda and beat on medium speed until completely combined. Remove the bowl from the mixer stand and fold the asparagus mixture into the cheese mixture with a rubber spatula until evenly combined. Transfer the mixture to the baking dish.

4. Bake until golden brown on top, about 15 minutes. Remove from the oven and let cool for at least 10 minutes before serving. Accompany with rye bread.

HERBED LARD AND PORK CRACKLINGS

GRIEBENSCHMALZBROT

GRIEBENSCHMALZ is one of the most common Brotzeit options in all of Germany, and it's particularly popular in Bavaria. Here, the flavor of this already very flavorful pork-fat spread is upped by infusing fresh bay leaves into the rendered lard before chilling it. If you don't have the time or space to make your own pork cracklings, crushed store-bought pork rinds *(chicharrones)* will work fine. You might be surprised to find that this snack eats much lighter than it reads on paper. Griebenschmalz also makes a good accompaniment to any cured-meat spread.

INGREDIENTS (SERVES 8)

2½ lb/1.2 kg fresh pork skin

1 lb/455 g lard

12 fresh bay leaves, sliced, or 6 dried bay leaves, crushed

4 sprigs fresh marjoram

1 tbsp kosher salt

½ tsp freshly ground black pepper

Hearty rye bread for serving

1. In a large pot, combine the pork skin with water to cover and bring to a boil over high heat. Lower the heat to a simmer and continue cooking, uncovered, until the skin is tender and the tip of a knife can easily be inserted into it, about 1 hour.

2. Using a slotted spoon, transfer the pork skin to a sheet pan and let cool completely. Let the cooking liquid cool to room temperature, then transfer to a jar or other container, cover, and refrigerate overnight.

3. Cut the cooled pork skin into ½-in/12-mm pieces, add to a medium saucepan, and place over medium-high heat. Cook, stirring occasionally, until the fat has rendered and the pieces are crisp and browned, about 1 hour. Using a slotted spoon, transfer the cracklings to a heatproof container, let cool, cover, and refrigerate overnight. Transfer the rendered fat to a separate heatpoof container, let cool, cover and refrigerate overnight.

4. The next day, remove the reserved pork skin cooking liquid from the refrigerator, scoop off the fat, and put the fat in a medium saucepan. (You can save the liquid for soup, pâté, or any recipe that calls for a gelatinous stock or aspic.) Add the fat from cooking the cracklings to the same pan along with the lard and bay leaves. Melt over medium heat, then cook until the lard is fully infused with the fragrance of bay, about 1 hour. Remove the pan from the heat and allow the lard to cool slightly, then strain through a fine-mesh sieve into a heatproof bowl. Discard the bay leaves.

5. Add the chopped marjoram and the cracklings to the lard and mix well. Let cool to room temperature, then cover and refrigerate overnight before serving.

6. Bring the spread to cool room temperature or serve it directly from the refrigerator. Season it with the salt and pepper and spread on slices of rye to serve.

SWEET-AND-SOUR PICKLED TROUT ROLLS

FORELLEN ROLLMOPS

UNLESS YOU LIVE BY THE NORTH SEA, high-quality fresh herring, which makes the best *Rollmops,* is hard to come by. Instead of using jarred pickled fish (too fishy), we use fresh trout for this version of quick-pickled fish popular in northern Germany and Scandinavia. Simply roll up each piece of fish, secure the roll with a toothpick, and leave in brine overnight. The next day, the rolls are ready to eat.

INGREDIENTS (SERVES 4)

PICKLING LIQUID

1½ cups/360 ml white wine vinegar

1½ cups/300 g sugar

1 tsp kosher salt

5 whole cloves

1 tbsp coriander seeds

½ bunch fresh dill

1 tbsp dill seeds

5 whole allspice berries

1 tsp yellow mustard seeds

1 carrot, peeled and sliced

1 shallot, sliced

½ small leek, white and green parts, sliced

4 trout fillets, about 4 oz/115 g each

1 dill pickle, about 6 in/15 cm long

1 white onion, thinly sliced

Sour cream for serving

Drained brine-cured capers for serving

Hearty rye bread for serving

1. *To make the pickling liquid,* in a medium saucepan, combine the vinegar, sugar, salt, cloves, coriander seeds, fresh dill, dill seeds, allspice, mustard seeds, carrot, shallot, and leek and bring to a boil over high heat. Immediately remove the pan from the heat and let the liquid cool to room temperature.

2. Cut each trout fillet in half lengthwise to create 8 long slices total. Cut each slice in half crosswise to create a total of 16 pieces of fish, each about 4 in/10 cm long. Cut the dill pickle into 16 slices roughly the same size as the trout pieces. Place a pickle slice and a few onion slices on each piece of fish, roll up the fish, and secure the roll with a toothpick.

3. Place the rolls in a large, widemouthed canning jar or other nonreactive container with a lid and pour in the pickling liquid to cover the rolls completely. Cap tightly and refrigerate overnight, or for up to 2 weeks.

4. Remove the rolls from the pickling liquid, arrange on a platter, and accompany with sour cream, capers, and rye bread. They can be served as rolls, or they can be opened up and used to make open-faced sandwiches.

BAKED SMOKED FISH SPREAD
WITH CAPERS
FISCHAUFSTRICH

SMOKED SEAFOOD SPREADS ARE POPULAR in northern Germany, which borders on the North and Baltic Seas and has a long-standing tradition of smoking foods to preserve them. For this Brotzeit, which can be served hot or cold (we prefer it hot), mashed potatoes are incorporated into a base of smoked trout and salmon to give the mixture a texture reminiscent of *brandade,* the creamy blend of salt cod, olive oil, and potatoes found in France and with variations and under other names in Spain, Portugal, and Italy. This spread differs in taste from *brandade,* however, because of its strong smoky profile and the bold natural flavors of trout and salmon.

INGREDIENTS (SERVES 4 TO 6)

Kosher salt

1 lb/455 g russet potatoes

4 tbsp unsalted butter

1 tbsp canola oil

1 shallot, minced

2 garlic cloves, minced

¼ cup/60 ml white wine

Grated zest and juice of 1 lemon

2 tsp sweet smoked Spanish paprika

2 tbsp finely chopped fresh dill

2 tbsp finely chopped fresh curly-leaf parsley

4 oz/115 g smoked trout fillet, flaked

4 oz/115 g smoked salmon, cut into ½-in/12-mm pieces

1 tbsp brined-cured capers, drained

¼ cup/25 g grated Parmesan cheese

⅓ cup/30 g panko bread crumbs

Rye or sourdough bread for serving

1. Fill a large pot two-thirds full with water, add enough salt for the water to taste like seawater, and bring to a boil over high heat. Slip the potatoes into the boiling water, return the water to a boil, adjust the heat to maintain a simmer, and cook until a knife inserted into a potato meets no resistance, 25 to 30 minutes.

2. Drain the potatoes into a colander and let cool just until they can be handled, then peel them. Pass the warm potatoes through a ricer held over a large bowl, or place the potatoes in the bowl and mash with a potato masher. The potatoes do not need to be smooth.

3. Preheat the oven to 400°F/200°C. Grease a small baking dish with 1 tbsp of the butter.

4. In a medium frying pan, combine the canola oil and 1 tbsp butter over medium heat. When the butter melts, add the shallot and garlic and cook, stirring, until the shallot is translucent, about 4 minutes. Add the wine, lemon zest and juice and cook, stirring occasionally, until the liquid has almost evaporated, about 4 minutes. Add the paprika, dill, and parsley. Stir well and remove the pan from the heat.

5. Pour the contents of the frying pan into the bowl with the potatoes and mix well. Fold the smoked trout, smoked salmon, and capers into the potato mixture, distributing them evenly. Transfer the mixture to the prepared baking dish, spreading it evenly and smoothing the top.

6. In a small saucepan, melt the remaining 2 tbsp butter over low heat, then immediately remove from the heat. In a small bowl, stir together the cheese, panko, and melted butter. Spread the mixture evenly over the top of the potato mixture.

7. Bake the spread until the top is nicely browned, about 25 minutes. Remove from the oven and let cool for 5 minutes. Serve directly from the baking dish accompanied with sliced bread.

BAVARIAN CHEESE SPREAD
OBATZDA

WHILE WORKING IN THE KITCHEN at Liederkranz in Reading, Jeremy mixed up enough Obatzda to last several drinking lifetimes, so it is no surprise that it's on the menu at Brauhaus Schmitz now. Although not widely known throughout Germany, this cheese-based snack, eaten with bread or soft pretzels, is a must in Bavarian beer gardens, where it's served in hefty scoops garnished with sliced raw onions. It's not an inherently spicy spread, but you can get it there by adding more hot paprika and chili powder to taste. The inclusion of *Butterkäse*, a common cow's milk cheese with a mild, accessible flavor and buttery appearance, helps achieve an even consistency. If you cannot find it, swap in an easy-going substitute like Muenster.

INGREDIENTS (SERVES 4)

½ cup/115 g unsalted butter, at room temperature

4 oz/115 g cream cheese, at room temperature

4 oz/115 g Brie cheese, cut into small pieces

8 oz/225 g Butterkäse, cut into small pieces

1½ tsp kosher salt

1 tsp Hungarian hot paprika

2 tsp Hungarian sweet paprika

1 tsp chili powder

½ tsp caraway seeds

½ white onion, minced

½ red onion, thinly sliced

4 red radishes, thinly sliced

1 tbsp finely chopped fresh curly-leaf parsley

Rye or sourdough bread for serving

1. In a food processor, combine the butter and cream cheese and process until smooth. Add the Brie and Butterkäse and process again until smooth. Add the salt, hot and sweet paprikas, chili powder, caraway seeds, and white onion and pulse until combined. Transfer to a bowl, cover, and refrigerate for at least 1 hour, or up to 1 week.

2. Serve the cheese spread garnished with the red onion, radishes, and parsley. Accompany with sliced bread.

SMOKED BEEF MARROWBONES
WITH PARSLEY-CORNICHON SALAD
KNOCHENMARK

THE MOST COMMON WAY Germans consume *Knochenmark*, or "bone marrow," is in a soup that floats rich marrow dumplings in beef consommé. This Brotzeit idea skews a little more brasserie, using canoe-cut marrowbones (split lengthwise; ask your butcher to cut them for you) that are brined and then hot smoked for big flavor.

INGREDIENTS (SERVES 4)

6 beef marrowbones, each about 6 in/15 cm long, canoe cut (see headnote)

Kosher salt

1 baguette, cut on the diagonal into slices ½ in/12 mm thick

SALAD

1 bunch fresh curly-leaf parsley, roughly chopped

½ cup/80 g cornichons, roughly chopped

1 shallot, minced

1 tsp white wine vinegar

2 tbsp olive oil

1 tsp freshly ground black pepper

Kosher salt

1. In a large pot or large, deep bowl, combine the marrowbones with water to cover and a big handful of salt, moving the bones around to dissolve the salt. Cover and refrigerate overnight, changing the water and adding another handful of salt at least twice. The next day, rinse the bones with cold water and then place on a sheet pan.

2. Following the manufacturer's instructions, preheat your smoker to 350°F/180°C. If using a charcoal or gas grill, prepare a medium-hot fire, then place presoaked wood chips in an aluminum-foil packet, poke a couple of holes in the packet, and place the packet directly on the hot coals of a charcoal grill or on a burner of a gas grill.

3. Place the marrowbones on the smoker or grill rack, cover, and cook until the marrow is just soft enough to be easily spread, about 20 minutes.

Check on it regularly, as the marrow can soften more quickly, depending on how hot your smoker or grill is.

4. When the marrowbones are ready, transfer them to individual serving plates and keep warm. Arrange the baguette slices on the smoker or grill rack and grill, turning once, until nicely etched with grill marks on both sides, about 2 minutes on each side.

5. *To make the salad,* in a medium bowl, combine the parsley, cornichons, shallot, vinegar, olive oil, and pepper and mix well. Season with salt. Let the salad sit at room temperature until serving.

6. Top the bones with the salad, dividing it evenly, and serve immediately with the grilled bread.

COLD-SMOKED VENISON CARPACCIO
WITH PICKLED OYSTER MUSHROOMS
REHCARPACCIO

YARDS, WHICH MAKES SOME OF THE BEST BEER IN PHILLY, has long been a friend and supporter of Brauhaus Schmitz. This carpaccio originates with a beer dinner we put together with the brewery in the early days of the restaurant. We wanted something that would pair well with Poor Richard's Tavern Spruce Ale, based on a recipe that can be traced back to Ben Franklin himself. After quick-curing lean, wonderfully gamey venison loin in a dry spice mix that contained juniper and allspice, we cold smoked the meat on an outdoor grill and thinly shaved it. The carpaccio is then dressed with olive oil and coarse sea salt and paired on the plate with pickled mushrooms, a good accompaniment for this *Jäger* (hunter) specialty.

INGREDIENTS (SERVES 8)

MUSHROOMS

1 lb/455 g oyster mushrooms

3 cups/720 ml white wine vinegar

1½ cups/360 ml water

1 tsp whole allspice

1 shallot, sliced

½ cup plus 1 tbsp/ 115 g granulated sugar

1 tbsp kosher salt

6 sprigs fresh thyme

1 tsp juniper berries

2 whole allspice berries

1 tsp black peppercorns

2 tbsp kosher salt

One 3½-lb/1.6-kg venison loin, silver skin and sinew removed

Coarse sea salt and freshly ground black pepper

Fresh curly-leaf parsley leaves, torn, for garnish

Extra-virgin olive oil for drizzling

1. *To prepare the mushrooms,* pull the mushroom clusters apart into bite-size pieces and trim the stems away. Place the mushrooms in a bowl or other container large enough to accommodate the mushrooms and the pickling liquid. In a medium saucepan, combine the vinegar, water, allspice, shallot, sugar, salt, and thyme and bring to a boil over high heat, stirring to dissolve the sugar. When the mixture boils, remove the pan from the heat. Let the mixture cool, then pour over the mushrooms, cover, and refrigerate for 3 days.

2. In a spice grinder, combine the juniper, all-spice, and peppercorns and pulse until coarsely ground. Transfer to a small bowl and stir in the kosher salt. Rub the spice mixture evenly over the venison loin, then place the loin in a container, cover, and refrigerate overnight, or up to 48 hours.

3. Remove the venison from the refrigerator, rinse off the curing mixture with cold water, and let come to room temperature. Meanwhile, soak a big handful of hickory wood chips in water to cover for about 30 minutes.

4. Drain the wood chips, place them on a sheet of aluminum foil, and wrap the foil around the chips, forming a packet. Poke some holes in the top of the packet, place the packet on a burner on the stove top, and turn the burner to high heat. When the packet starts to smolder and smoke heavily, place it underneath the grill rack in an unlit grill with a lid. Place the venison loin directly on the grill rack, close the lid of the grill, and cold-smoke the venison for 1½ hours.

5. Remove the venison from the grill, wrap it in plastic wrap, and place in the freezer for 1 hour. The meat should be firm but not frozen.

6. Slice the venison against the grain as thinly as possible and arrange on a serving plate. Using a slotted spoon, lift the mushrooms from their brine and arrange on top of the venison slices. Sprinkle with sea salt and pepper, garnish with parsley, drizzle with olive oil, and then serve.

HEADCHEESE

PRESSKOPF

YOU WILL NEED A LARGE STOCKPOT to hold the pig's head and feet, pork shoulder, water, wine, and seasonings. It is important that you not season the stock until it has reduced enough to firm up. If you season it too early, you can end up with a reduced stock that tastes too salty.

This recipe makes more headcheese than you will need for the headcheese salad on page 45. It is good thinly sliced and served on a charcuterie board or alongside a simple salad of mixed lettuces dressed with olive oil and lemon juice.

INGREDIENTS (MAKES ABOUT 5 LB/2.3 KG)

1 tbsp whole allspice

2 tbsp black peppercorns

2 tbsp yellow mustard seeds

1 whole pig's head

2 whole pig's feet

One 3-lb/1.4-kg bone-in pork shoulder

2 yellow onions, cut in half

1 leek, white and green parts, cut in half

1 carrot, peeled

1 head garlic, unpeeled, cut in half

6 fresh bay leaves, or 3 dried bay leaves

4 qt/3.8 L water

2 cups/480 ml dry white wine

1 synthetic bologna casing, 24 in/61 cm long and 4⅞ in/ 12 cm in diameter, soaked in water to cover for 30 minutes and drained (optional)

1 tbsp kosher salt

¼ tsp freshly ground black pepper

1 tbsp chopped fresh curly-leaf parsley

1. In a small, dry frying pan, combine the allspice, peppercorns, and mustard seeds and toast over medium heat, stirring the spices or shaking the pan often, until fragrant, about 2 minutes. Pour the spices into a small bowl and let cool, then wrap them in a piece of cheesecloth and tie the corners together with kitchen string.

2. In a large stockpot, combine the pig's head, pig's feet, pork shoulder, onions, leek, carrot, garlic, bay leaves, water, and wine. Bring to a boil over high heat and use a spoon to skim off and discard any foam from the top. Add the spice bag, lower the heat to a simmer, cover, and cook, lifting the lid occasionally and using a spoon to skim off and discard any foam from the surface, until all of the meats are tender, about 3½ hours.

3. Remove the pot from the heat. Lift out the head, feet, and shoulder and set aside to cool until they can be handled. Strain the liquid through a fine-mesh sieve into a container. Measure 8 cups/ 2 L of the liquid and pour into a medium sauce-pan. (Reserve the remaining liquid for another use or discard.) Place the saucepan over high heat, bring to a boil, and cook, stirring occasionally, until reduced by half, about 45 minutes.

4. While the liquid is reducing, pull the meat, fat, and skin off of the head, feet, and shoulder, discarding any bones and tough gristle. Roughly chop the meat, fat, and skin and set aside. Line the bottom and sides of two 4½-by-12-in/11.5-by-30-cm terrine molds with plastic wrap, allowing the plastic wrap to overhang the sides by at least 3 in/7.5 cm, or have ready the bologna casing. Spoon the meat mixture into the mold or casing.

5. When the liquid has reduced by half, scoop out 1 tbsp into a small container and refrigerate it for 15 minutes. The liquid should set firmly like gelatin. If it doesn't, return the liquid to the stove top and continue reducing for another 15 minutes or so, then test again. Season the liquid with the salt and pepper, then stir in the parsley. Pour the liquid over the meat mixture in the mold or casing. Fold the plastic wrap over the top to cover, or tie off the casing with kitchen string. Refrigerate overnight. The headcheese can be stored in the refrigerator for up to 1 week.

HEADCHEESE SALAD
WITH MUSTARD DRESSING, RED ONION, AND DILL PICKLE
FLEISCHSALAT

SIMILAR IN MAKEUP to a typical chicken or tuna salad, this best-served-cold Brotzeit offering relies on flavor-packed *Presskopf,* or "headcheese." Of course, if you are short on time, you can purchase headcheese at any butcher shop or delicatessen that carries high-quality German products. Make sure to opt for meatier "white" headcheese without aspic, as the gelatin tends to melt and turn the salad watery.

You can also substitute *coppa di testa,* or Italian headcheese. If you find headcheese altogether unappealing, you can swap in bologna, but any fan of charcuterie and offal should give this salad a chance.

INGREDIENTS (SERVES 4 TO 6)

DRESSING

½ cup/120 ml mayonnaise

½ cup/120 ml whole-grain mustard, homemade (see page 196) or store-bought

2 tbsp cider vinegar

4 sprigs fresh curly-leaf parsley, minced

8 oz/225 g white head-cheese, homemade (see page 42) or store-bought, thinly sliced

½ red onion, thinly sliced

1 dill pickle, about 6 in/ 15 cm long, chopped

Hearty rye bread for serving

1. *To make the dressing,* in a small bowl, stir together the mayonnaise, mustard, vinegar, and parsley, mixing well.

2. In a medium bowl, combine the headcheese, onion, and pickle. Add the dressing and, using your hands, mix together to coat evenly.

3. To serve, spoon the salad onto sliced rye. Store any leftover salad in an airtight container in the refrigerator for up to 1 week.

ESCARGOTS
WITH HAZELNUT-RAMP BUTTER
SCHNECKEN IN HASELNUSS-BÄRLAUCH-BUTTER

THE CLASSIC COMBINATION of butter, garlic, and snails, which most of us readily associate with Gallic cooking, goes German with this simple preparation. *Schnecken* are commonly eaten in the country's densely wooded regions, most frequently in *Schneckensuppe*, a cream-based sliced snail soup. This recipe takes the snails out of the bowl and puts them onto bread. *Bärlauch* (bear leeks), or ramps, also known as wild garlic or wild leeks, appear in early spring in the United States and the season is extremely short. If you cannot find ramps, substitute three green onions, white and green parts, and two garlic cloves.

You will need only one-fourth of the flavored butter for this recipe. It is especially delicious on spaetzle or can be used almost any time an herbed butter is called for.

INGREDIENTS (SERVES 4)

HAZELNUT-RAMP BUTTER

½ cup/70 g blanched hazelnuts

1 lb/455 g unsalted butter, at room temperature

6 ramps, bulbs and leaves, minced

Grated zest and juice of 1 lemon

2 tsp kosher salt

1 tsp freshly ground black pepper

One 12 oz/340 g can escargots, drained and rinsed

1 leek, white and green parts, diced

2 cups/480 ml beef or chicken stock

Toasted hearty rye bread for serving

1. *To make the butter,* preheat the oven to 350°F/180°C. Spread the hazelnuts on a sheet pan and toast until golden brown, about 20 minutes. Remove from the oven, let cool, and chop coarsely.

2. In a food processor or a blender, combine the hazelnuts, butter, ramps, lemon zest and juice, salt, and pepper and mix until thoroughly combined. The nuts should still be a bit chunky.

3. Lay a sheet of waxed paper on a work surface. Scoop the butter mixture onto the paper, spreading it in a lengthwise strip on the sheet and leaving about 1 in/2.5 cm uncovered on each end. Roll the paper around the butter, pressing against the paper lightly to shape the butter into a long, even cylinder. Grasp the ends and twist in opposite directions to seal closed. Refrigerate the butter until needed, up to 2 weeks (or freeze for up to 2 months).

4. In a medium saucepan, combine the escargots, leek, and stock and bring to a boil over medium-high heat. Lower the heat to a simmer and cook until the liquid is reduced by three-fourths, about 30 minutes. Remove the pan from the heat and quickly whisk in one-fourth of the hazelnut butter, 1 tbsp at a time, until the mixture has thickened.

5. Serve immediately spooned onto slices of toasted rye.

2

SALADS

SALATE

"YOU HAVE SALADS ON THE MENU? But Germans don't eat salads!" We cannot even begin to count the number of times we've heard this from customers at Brauhaus Schmitz. The belief that Germany is a nation that subsists on nothing but sausage and beer is perhaps the biggest misconception Americans have about German cooking. The reality is that German cuisine is just as balanced, seasonal, and well rounded as that of any of its European neighbors, a fact verified by the wealth of salads served throughout the country.

You'll find salads of all types on restaurant menus, but the tradition is just as strong away from public dining rooms. Germans are avid gardeners, their green thumbs put to work at community allotments and private plots alike. If they have a yard, they have a garden, though a plot of soil is not always a requirement for having a garden. Beate Green, the operations manager at Brauhaus Schmitz, has a tremendous array of vegetables growing on the balcony of her city apartment. She does wonders with tomatoes, lettuces, and green beans—the perfect raw material for satisfying salad preparations, and just a few of the most commonly cultivated vegetables back in her home country.

The recipes that follow are all based on traditional German salads, with *Löwenzahn* (dandelion greens), *Rettich* (radish), and *Spargel* (asparagus) being just a few of the most recognizable bases. And yes, we do share our take on the classic German potato salad, which is different from its American counterpart. In place of the heavy mayonnaise-based dressing typical of many American-style potato salads, German cooks commonly dress their potato salads with a simple herb-flavored vinaigrette. And there's very little meat used in German salads, where the focus is primarily, though not exclusively, on greens, green vegetables, and sometimes peppers, tomatoes, and radishes. We have, however, slipped a warm salad of potatoes, squash, mushrooms, and roasted chicken into the mix.

Because most German salads star vegetables, it is important to keep both quality and seasonality in mind when cooking your way through this chapter. Even the best-executed recipe will turn out poorly if you're not starting with the freshest in-season ingredients. Whether you are on the hunt for a light lunch or looking for a side for an impromptu barbecue or weeknight supper, you'll find a German-inspired salad here to fit your menu. We have simplified assembly and serving, too, by making all of the salads family-style, which allows you to assemble, dress, garnish, and serve nearly them all of them from the same bowl in which they are tossed.

DANDELION GREEN SALAD
WITH WARM BACON–MUSTARD SEED VINAIGRETTE
LÖWENZAHNSALAT

ONE OF THE MOST UBIQUITOUS and celebrated greens in all of Germany, *Löwenzahn*, or dandelion, is synonymous with spring. (It's also the name of a popular German children's television program, similar to *Sesame Street*.) Dandelion greens, whether foraged or purchased by the bunch at a farmers' market, are a flavorful salad base, with a slight bitterness that stands up to any addition. Soon after Jeremy and his family moved into their new house in Reading, Pennsylvania, a neighbor, an old Pennsylvania Dutch woman, went into their backyard and began picking weeds. His dad asked the woman what she was doing. She said she was picking dandelion greens to make salad, and she described the hot bacon dressing. This recipe is a version of that popular Pennsylvania Dutch salad. The hot bacon dressing, its fattiness cut with vinegar, mustard, and brown sugar, wilts the greens to create an appealing textural contrast with the lardons and croutons.

INGREDIENTS (SERVES 4)

CROUTONS

2 slices pumpernickel bread, cut into ½-in/12-mm cubes

2 tbsp unsalted butter, melted

1 tbsp kosher salt

DRESSING

1 lb/455 g thick-cut bacon, cut into pieces 1 in/2.5 cm wide

1 small shallot, thinly sliced

2 garlic cloves, thinly sliced

2 tbsp cider vinegar

3 tbsp firmly packed dark brown sugar

2 tbsp whole-grain mustard, homemade (see page 196) or store-bought

3 tbsp grapeseed or canola oil

1 large bunch dandelion greens, about 12 oz/340 g, trimmed and cut into bite-size pieces

1. *To make the croutons,* preheat the oven to 350°F/180°C. Put the pumpernickel cubes in a medium bowl, drizzle with the butter, sprinkle with the salt, and toss to coat the cubes evenly. Spread the cubes on a sheet pan and bake until they are firm but not completely hard, about 20 minutes. Remove from the oven and let cool.

2. *To make the dressing,* in a medium frying pan, fry the bacon over medium-high heat until lightly browned, about 5 minutes. Drain off the bacon fat from the pan into a small heatproof bowl and reserve for another use. Turn the heat to low, add the shallot and garlic, and cook, stirring, until translucent, about 2 minutes. Add the vinegar and brown sugar and stir until thoroughly combined. Remove the pan from the heat, whisk in the mustard, and then slowly whisk in the grape-seed oil until emulsified.

3. Put the dandelion greens in a large bowl. Pour the warm dressing over the dandelion greens and toss until wilted. Serve immediately, topped with the croutons.

KALE SALAD
WITH PAPRIKA-DUSTED HAZELNUTS AND MUSTARD VINAIGRETTE
GRÜNEKOHLSALAT

KALE CAME INTO CULINARY VOGUE in the United States relatively recently, but it's always been eaten in Germany, especially in the country's colder northern regions. One of the most common preparations features *Pinkel,* a fatty pork sausage studded with buckwheat groats, served atop braised kale. This recipe keeps the greens raw, but requires you to massage the dressing into the leaves to break them down. A generous helping of grated Gouda and paprika-seasoned hazelnuts provides nice pops of salt and crunch. Don't be off-put by the inclusion of Maggi seasoning sauce in this recipe. Invented by a German-speaking Swiss of Italian ancestry, it is a widely used wheat-based sauce comparable to soy sauce.

INGREDIENTS (SERVES 4)

HAZELNUTS

1 cup/135 g blanched hazelnuts

1 tsp hot or sweet smoked Spanish paprika

½ tsp grapeseed or vegetable oil

½ tsp kosher salt

DRESSING

1 garlic clove, minced

2 tbsp Löwensenf or Dijon spicy mustard

2 tsp Maggi seasoning sauce

Grated zest and juice of ½ lemon

Leaves from 6 sprigs fresh thyme

1 tsp freshly cracked black pepper

2 tbsp grapeseed or olive oil

1 large bunch kale, about 12 oz/340 g, leaves and stems cut into bite-size pieces

1 small shallot, sliced

4 oz/115 g aged Gouda or Prima Donna cheese, grated

Freshly ground black pepper

1. *To prepare the hazelnuts,* preheat the oven to 350°F/180°C. In a small bowl, combine the hazelnuts, paprika, grapeseed oil, and salt and toss to coat the nuts evenly. Spread the nuts in a single layer on a sheet pan and toast in the oven until brownish red and fragrant, about 15 minutes. Remove from the oven, let the nuts cool completely, then crush the cooled nuts lightly so they are easier to eat in the salad. Set aside.

2. *To make the dressing,* in a blender, combine the garlic, mustard, Maggi sauce, lemon zest and juice, thyme, and pepper and turn the blender on to low speed. When the ingredients begin incorporating, increase the blender speed to medium, then slowly drizzle in the grapeseed oil and blend until emulsified. Set aside.

3. In a large bowl, combine the kale and shallot. Pour the dressing over the kale and mix it in well, using your hands to "massage" the kale with the dressing until it is soft and slightly wilted. Garnish with the hazelnuts, Gouda, and pepper and serve immediately.

KOHLRABI SALAD
WITH BLACK GARLIC–
SOUR CREAM DRESSING
KOHLRABISALAT

JUST HOW GERMAN IS KOHLRABI? There's simply no alternative English name for this sturdy member of the hardy, healthful brassica clan whose name translates to "cabbage turnip." Eaten throughout Germany, kohlrabi is prepared both raw (tasting similar to a radish or turnip) and cooked (comparable to broccoli stems). When eaten raw, it is most often grated and used in a salad that closely resembles coleslaw. Here, the bulbous vegetable is cut into cubes and tossed with a sour cream–based dressing flavored with a distinctive and not-very-German ingredient: black garlic. Used frequently in Korean food and in other Asian cuisines, black garlic is a milder, sweeter alternative to raw garlic that achieves its unique color and texture through fermentation. If you cannot find black garlic, substitute garlic confit or roasted garlic.

INGREDIENTS (SERVES 4 TO 6)

DRESSING

½ cup/120 ml sour cream

¼ cup/60 ml mayonnaise

5 black garlic cloves, minced

Grated zest and juice of
1 lemon

1 tsp kosher salt

1 lb/455 g kohlrabi

1 cup/30 g baby spinach

¼ cup/25 g grated carrot

1 cup/55 g crispy fried
onions, homemade or
store-bought

1. *To make the dressing,* in a small bowl, whisk together the sour cream, mayonnaise, black garlic, lemon zest and juice, and salt until well mixed. Set aside.

2. Using a vegetable peeler, remove the tough outer layer of each kohlrabi bulb. Cut the bulbs into 1-in/2.5-cm cubes and place in a large bowl.

Add the spinach and carrot, pour the dressing over the top, and stir together until the vegetables are evenly coated.

3. Garnish with the fried onions and serve immediately.

ROASTED PARSNIP SALAD
WITH HAZELNUTS, BLUE CHEESE, AND WHEAT BEER VINAIGRETTE
PASTINAKENSALAT

THIS DISH STARS PARSNIPS, an easy-to-work-with alternative to beets or butternut squash in a winter salad. Typically used in soups and salads in Germany, the parsnips are roasted here, bringing out a natural sweetness that marries well with the pleasantly bitter frisée and the salty pumpernickel bread crumbs. The dressing incorporates *Hefeweizen* (malted-wheat beer), a little shout-out to German beer and its versatility in the kitchen.

INGREDIENTS (SERVES 4)

PARSNIPS

4 parsnips, peeled and cut into coins ½ in/12 mm thick

1 shallot, sliced

1 tbsp grapeseed or canola oil

1 tsp kosher salt

Freshly cracked black pepper

Leaves from 4 sprigs fresh thyme

PUMPERNICKEL CRUMBS

2 slices pumpernickel bread

1 tbsp unsalted butter, melted

Pinch of kosher salt (optional)

HAZELNUTS

1 cup/135 g blanched hazelnuts

1 tsp hot or sweet smoked Spanish paprika

½ tsp grapeseed or canola oil

½ tsp kosher salt

DRESSING

2 tbsp malt vinegar

2 tbsp wheat beer, preferably Hefeweizen

1 tbsp honey

1 small shallot, minced

½ tsp kosher salt

¼ cup/60 ml grapeseed oil

2 red radishes, cut into matchsticks

1 small head red oak-leaf lettuce, cut into bite-size pieces

1 small head frisée, cut into bite-size pieces

Kosher salt and freshly ground black pepper

4 oz/115 g Bavarian blue or similar creamy blue cheese, crumbled

1 tbsp pumpkin seed oil

1. *To roast the parsnips,* preheat the oven to 350°F/180°C. In a bowl, combine the parsnips, shallot, grapeseed oil, salt, a few grinds of pepper, and the thyme and toss until the parsnips are evenly coated. Transfer to a sheet pan, spread in a single layer, and roast until easily pierced with the tip of a knife, 15 to 20 minutes. Remove from the oven and let cool to room temperature. Leave the oven on.

(Continued)

2. *To prepare the pumpernickel crumbs,* tear the bread into pieces, drop the pieces into a food processor, and pulse until coarse crumbs form. In a small bowl, combine the crumbs, butter, and salt (if using) and toss to coat the crumbs evenly. Spread the crumbs on a sheet pan and toast in the 350°F/180°C oven until crunchy, about 15 minutes. Remove from the oven and let cool to room temperature. Leave the oven on. (The crumbs can be stored in an airtight container at room temperature for up to 2 weeks.)

3. *To prepare the hazelnuts,* in a small bowl, combine the hazelnuts, paprika, grapeseed oil, and salt and toss to coat the nuts evenly. Spread the nuts in a single layer on a sheet pan and toast in the 350°F/180°C oven until brownish red and fragrant, about 15 minutes. Remove from the oven, let the nuts cool completely, then crush the cooled nuts lightly so they are easier to eat in the salad. Set aside.

4. *To make the dressing,* in a small bowl, whisk together the vinegar, beer, honey, shallot, and salt. Slowly whisk in the grapeseed oil until emulsified.

5. In a large bowl, combine the parsnips, radishes, lettuce, and frisée. Pour in half of the dressing and toss to coat all of the vegetables evenly. Taste and add more dressing if needed. (Any leftover dressing can be stored in an airtight container in the refrigerator for up to 1 week.) Season with salt and pepper and toss again.

6. Top the salad with the pumpernickel crumbs, blue cheese, and hazelnuts. Drizzle with the pumpkin seed oil and serve immediately.

RADISH SALAD
WITH CUCUMBER, WATERCRESS, ORANGE SEGMENTS, AND SHEEP'S MILK CHEESE
RETTICHSALAT

RADISH SALADS are common throughout Germany, but our new German *Rettichsalat* takes a few stylistic liberties. For starters, we use three types of radish: the common red radish, the mildly spicy daikon (a good stand-in for the White Icicle radish), and the colorful watermelon radish, which is visually appealing and sweet. The natural bite of the radishes is balanced by fresh basil, orange segments, and a simple citrus dressing.

INGREDIENTS (SERVES 6)

DRESSING

Juice of 2 oranges

1 tbsp honey

½ cup/120 ml cider vinegar

2 tbsp finely chopped fresh basil

½ cup/120 ml grapeseed or canola oil

3 green onions

Grapeseed or canola oil for the grill pan

4 red radishes, trimmed and quartered lengthwise

One 6-in/15-cm piece daikon, peeled and thinly sliced crosswise

1 watermelon radish, peeled and thinly sliced crosswise

1 English cucumber, halved lengthwise, seeded, and sliced crosswise into half-moons ½ in/12 mm thick

1 lb/455 g watercress, coarsely chopped

2 oranges, peeled, segmented, and seeded

12 fresh basil leaves

4-oz/115-g piece aged sheep's milk cheese, such as pecorino romano

I. *To make the dressing,* in a small saucepan, combine the orange juice, honey, and vinegar over medium-high heat. Bring to a boil and cook until reduced by half. Remove the pan from the heat and let the mixture cool completely. Stir in the basil, then slowly whisk in the grapeseed oil until emulsified. Set aside.

2. Trim off the root end and ½ in/12 mm from the tops of the green onions. Preheat a stove-top ridged grill pan over medium-high heat and oil the pan. Place the green onions on the hot pan and cook, turning as needed, until lightly grilled on all sides, about 5 minutes. Remove from the heat, let cool, and cut into 2-in/5-cm pieces.

3. In a large bowl, combine the red radishes, daikon, watermelon radish, cucumber, watercress, grilled green onions, orange segments, and basil leaves and toss to mix well. Whisk the dressing briefly, then pour over the salad and toss to coat all of the ingredients evenly.

4. Grate the cheese over the top of the salad and serve immediately.

WHITE ASPARAGUS SALAD
WITH FRISÉE, CHERRY TOMATOES, AND AGED GOUDA VINAIGRETTE
SPARGELSALAT

EVERY YEAR, Brauhaus Schmitz runs a *Spargelfest* celebration throughout the month of May, featuring a wide and ever-changing variety of dishes celebrating Germany's most popular warm-weather vegetable. We've done nearly everything with it, from stuffing it inside a roasting chicken to puréeing it for a crème brûlée base. This salad, the goal of which is to highlight the natural flavor of white asparagus, is much simpler. (Although common in the United States, green asparagus is served only rarely in Germany.) The key to success for this dish is attention to detail when handling the raw spears and taking care not to overcook them.

INGREDIENTS (SERVES 2 TO 4)

DRESSING

¼ cup/30 g grated aged Gouda or Prima Donna cheese

1 tbsp white wine vinegar

½ tbsp kosher salt

1 tbsp finely chopped fresh chives

2 tbsp grapeseed or canola oil

1 tbsp extra-virgin olive oil

1 lb/455 g white asparagus

Kosher salt

½ cup/25 g coarsely chopped frisée

6 cherry tomatoes, quartered lengthwise

1 small shallot, sliced

¼ cup/30 g grated aged Gouda or Prima Donna cheese

1. *To make the dressing,* whisk together the cheese, vinegar, salt, and chives. Slowly whisk in the grapeseed oil and olive oil until emulsified. Set aside.

2. Using a vegetable peeler, peel each asparagus spear from just below the tip to the base, removing the tough skin. Snap off the woody base from each spear where it breaks easily and then even the ends with a paring knife.

3. Fill a medium saucepan two-thirds full with water, bring to a boil over high heat, and season with salt. It should not be too salty; instead, it should be seasoned just enough to resemble a good chicken stock. While the water is heating, ready an ice-water bath in a large bowl and line a plate with paper towels. Place both near the stove.

4. Plunge the asparagus into the boiling water and cook until tender, 8 to 10 minutes; the timing depends on the size of the asparagus. Using a wire skimmer or tongs, transfer the asparagus to the ice-water bath, immersing the spears completely. Leave them in the ice bath until chilled, about 5 minutes. Remove the spears from the ice bath and drain well on the towel-lined plate.

5. In a large bowl, combine the asparagus, frisée, tomatoes, and shallot. Pour in the dressing and toss to coat all of the ingredients evenly. Garnish with the cheese and serve immediately.

GREEN BEAN SALAD
WITH WHITE BEANS, TOMATOES, AND PINE NUTS
BOHNENSALAT

IN GERMANY, bean salads of this type are often made with a jarred mixed-bean mixture, but the combination of fresh green beans and high-quality canned white beans yields a more satisfying flavor and crunch. What also sets this recipe apart from other green bean salads is its bold dressing. Its key ingredient is sweet smoked Spanish paprika, which, when used properly, amplifies the more nuanced flavors of the other ingredients.

INGREDIENTS (SERVES 4 TO 6)

DRESSING

1 small shallot, minced

¼ cup/60 ml cider vinegar

1 tsp honey

1 tbsp finely chopped fresh tarragon

2 tsp sweet smoked Spanish paprika

1 tsp kosher salt

½ cup/120 ml grapeseed or canola oil

Kosher salt

8 oz/225 g green beans, ends trimmed

One 15-oz/430-g can cannellini or navy beans, rinsed and well drained

6 cherry tomatoes, quartered lengthwise

1 shallot, sliced

½ cup/80 g diced roasted red pepper

½ cup/70 g pine nuts, toasted

1. *To make the dressing,* in a small bowl, whisk together the shallot, vinegar, honey, tarragon, paprika, and salt. Slowly whisk in the grapeseed oil until emulsified. Set aside.

2. Fill a medium saucepan two-thirds full with water, bring to a boil over high heat, and season with salt. It should not be too salty; instead, it should be seasoned just enough to resemble a good chicken stock. While the water is heating, ready an ice-water bath in a large bowl and line a plate with paper towels. Place both near the stove.

3. Plunge the green beans into the boiling water and cook until very tender, about 7 minutes. Using a wire skimmer or slotted spoon, transfer the green beans to the ice-water bath, immersing them completely. Leave them in the ice bath until chilled, about 5 minutes. Remove the beans from the ice bath and drain well on the towel-lined plate.

4. In a large bowl, combine the green beans, cannellini beans, tomatoes, shallot, and red pepper. Pour in the dressing and toss to coat all of the ingredients evenly. Garnish with the pine nuts and serve immediately.

HEIRLOOM TOMATO SALAD
WITH TARRAGON VINAIGRETTE AND GOAT CHEESE
TOMATENSALAT

IF YOU HAVE EVER EATEN excellent heirloom tomatoes, you know that you don't have to do much to them to bring out their best qualities. Although this salad calls for more than just a light sprinkle of sea salt, it keeps the tomatoes at the forefront. The straight-forward tarragon vinaigrette lends a bright, warm, slightly anisey personality to this variation on a classic late-summer salad. Keep quality in mind when picking tomatoes for this dish. Pass up typical supermarket specimens, especially out of season. When you've finished the salad, don't toss out the liquid left at the bottom of the platter. It makes a tasty ready-made dressing for another salad.

INGREDIENTS (SERVES 4 TO 6)

DRESSING

1 small shallot, minced

1 tbsp cider vinegar

2 tsp honey

½ tsp kosher salt

1 tbsp finely chopped fresh tarragon

1 tbsp grapeseed or canola oil

1 tbsp pumpkin seed oil

4 large heirloom tomatoes, cut into slices and chunks

2 tbsp roasted pumpkin seeds (pepitas)

8 leaves Bibb or other butterhead lettuce, torn

4 oz/115 g fresh goat cheese, crumbled

Coarse sea salt and freshly ground black pepper

1. *To make the dressing,* in a small bowl, whisk together the shallot, vinegar, honey, salt, and tarragon until combined. Slowly whisk in the grapeseed and pumpkin seed oil until emulsified. Set aside.

2. In a large bowl, combine the tomatoes and pumpkin seeds. Pour the dressing over the tomato mixture and toss to coat the ingredients evenly. Arrange the lettuce on a platter and top with the tomato mixture, including the dressing. Scatter the cheese over the tomato mixture and sprinkle with salt and pepper. Serve immediately.

POTATO AND CUCUMBER SALAD
WITH DILL VINAIGRETTE
KARTOFFEL-GURKENSALAT

FOR THIS DISH, one of the most popular salads we do at Brauhaus Schmitz, we've combined two of Germany's most popular sides, potato salad and cucumber salad, into one. (Let this serve as the definitive reminder that German potato salad *never* contains mayonnaise or bacon!) The contrasting textures here are irresistible: warm, tender cooked fingerlings versus cool, crunchy raw cucumber. It's a versatile dish for a barbecue or cookout. Be sure to mix the salad while the fingerlings are still warm, as the starch of the potatoes combined with the vinaigrette helps to create a creamy consistency without the addition of added fat. If you cannot find fingerlings, replace them with another waxy potato, such as Yukon gold.

INGREDIENTS (SERVES 4 TO 6)

DRESSING

2 tbsp finely chopped fresh dill

½ cup/120 ml cider vinegar

1 tbsp whole-grain mustard, homemade (see page 196) or store-bought

1 tsp kosher salt

½ tsp freshly ground black pepper

½ cup/120 ml grapeseed or canola oil

2 lb/910 g fingerling potatoes

Kosher salt

2 large English cucumbers, halved lengthwise and sliced crosswise into half-moons ¼ in/6 mm thick

½ yellow onion, finely diced

1. *To make the dressing,* in a small bowl, whisk together the dill, vinegar, mustard, salt, and pepper. Slowly whisk in the grapeseed oil until emulsified. Set aside.

2. In a large saucepan, combine the potatoes with water to cover generously and season with salt. The water should not be too salty; instead, it should be seasoned just enough to resemble a good chicken stock. Bring the water to a boil over high heat, turn the heat to medium, and simmer until the potatoes can be easily pierced with the tip of a knife, about 25 minutes. Drain the potatoes and then spread them out on a sheet pan to cool slightly, about 10 minutes.

3. Cut the warm potatoes in half lengthwise. In a large bowl, combine the potatoes, cucumbers, and onion. Pour in the dressing and toss to coat all of the ingredients evenly. Serve immediately.

ROASTED CHICKEN, PORCINI, POTATO, AND SQUASH SALAD
WITH SMOKED BARLEY MALT
GEFLÜGELSALAT

AN EXCELLENT WAY TO USE UP THE LEFTOVERS from a whole roasted bird, this chicken salad gets its German identity from the addition of smoked barley malt, a play on what is used to brew traditional *Rauchbier*, or "smoked beer." (Look for smoked barley malt at home-brewing supply stores or online.) The trio of mushrooms, potatoes, and squash forms an earthy base for this warm, filling salad. If the chicken has crisp skin, be sure to use the skin, as it will add some salty, fatty goodness to the dish.

INGREDIENTS (SERVES 4 TO 6)

DRESSING

1 garlic clove, minced

2 tbsp finely chopped fresh curly-leaf parsley

1 tsp kosher salt

2 tsp white wine vinegar

1 tbsp spicy mustard, homemade (see page 197) or store-bought (such as Löwensenf or Dijon)

6 tbsp/90 ml grapeseed oil

SMOKED MALT SEASONING

½ cup/100 g smoked barley malt

2 tsp freshly ground black pepper

2 tsp coriander seeds

1 tsp red pepper flakes

1 tsp hot smoked Spanish paprika

2 tsp sweet Hungarian paprika

2 tsp kosher salt

2 tbsp dried onion flakes

2 tbsp dried garlic flakes

2 tbsp grapeseed or canola oil, plus more as needed

3 porcini or portobello mushrooms, trimmed and sliced

1½ cups/170 g peeled and cubed kabocha squash (¼-in/6-mm cubes)

1½ cups/225 g peeled and cubed Yukon gold potatoes (¼-in/6-mm cubes)

1 head frisée, roughly chopped

½ cup/35 g shredded red cabbage

½ cup/20 g roughly chopped watercress

3 cups/455 g coarsely shredded roasted chicken, cold

1. *To make the dressing,* in a small bowl, whisk together the garlic, parsley, salt, vinegar, and mustard. Slowly whisk in the grapeseed oil until emulsified. Set aside.

2. *To make the seasoning,* in a small food processor or a spice grinder, combine the smoked barley, black pepper, coriander seeds, red pepper flakes, hot and sweet paprikas, salt, dried onion flakes, and dried garlic flakes and pulse until coarsely ground. Set aside. (The seasoning can be stored in an airtight container in a cool, dark place for up to 3 months.)

3. Line two plates with paper towels. In a medium sauté pan, heat the grapeseed oil over high heat. When the oil is hot, add the mushrooms and cook, stirring occasionally, until nicely browned, about 3 minutes. Using a slotted spoon, transfer the mushrooms to a towel-lined plate. Turn the heat to medium, add the squash and potato cubes to the pan, and cook, stirring often and adding more oil to the pan if needed to prevent sticking, until lightly browned and tender, about 15 minutes. Using the slotted spoon, transfer the squash and potato cubes to the second towel-lined plate.

4. In a large bowl, combine the still-warm mushrooms, squash, and potatoes with the frisée, cabbage, and watercress and toss to mix. Pour in the dressing and toss to coat the vegetables evenly. Top the salad with the chicken and sprinkle the smoked malt seasoning evenly over the top. Serve immediately.

3

SOUPS

SUPPEN

AS IS THE CASE WITH MOST European cooking canons, soups have always provided honest nourishment for German families. Whether we're talking *Mehlsuppe*, a bare-bones peasant dish of water or stock thickened with toasted flour, or an elaborate fifty-ingredient soup for a Hessian wedding celebration, broth-based dishes are integral to German cooking and to Brauhaus Schmitz, as well.

The recipes in this chapter are built with traditional German ingredients and dressed up with contemporary touches. Aside from the strictly seasonal explorations here—barley and wild mushrooms for *Herbst* (fall); asparagus and morels for *Frühling* (spring)—we have focused on cooking with beer, producing some rustic, approachable bowls that can work on their own or as part of a multicourse dinner. There's even a hugely flavorful vegan option—yes, it's possible!

MUSHROOM AND SAUERKRAUT GOULASH

PILZGULASCH

VEGETARIAN DIETS are much more common in Germany than many might think, and there are plenty of everyday dishes—spaetzle, salads, many soups—that are traditionally meat-free. This soup is actually vegan, but only by accident. In experimenting with the dish, it turned out that sautéing the hefty base of vegetables in butter yielded a greasy final product, so the butter was swapped out for canola oil. The real flavor of this rich, Hungarian-inspired goulash is amped up by a large helping of sweet paprika. German and eastern European cooks know that paprika is much more than just a colorful garnish.

INGREDIENTS (SERVES 4 TO 6)

2 tbsp canola oil

2 stalks celery, diced

1 large carrot, peeled and diced

1 large yellow onion, diced

2 Yukon gold potatoes, diced

1 lb/455 g cremini mushrooms, trimmed and sliced

8 oz/225 g shiitake mushrooms, stemmed and sliced

8 oz/225 g portobello mushrooms, trimmed and sliced

8 oz/225 g oyster mushrooms, trimmed and sliced

6 garlic cloves, minced

½ cup/75 g sweet Hungarian paprika

2 tbsp kosher salt

1 tsp freshly ground black pepper

Leaves from 6 sprigs fresh thyme

2 cups/480 ml dry or medium-dry red wine

4 cups/960 ml water

1 lb/455 g sauerkraut, homemade (see page 194) or store-bought, drained

2 tbsp finely chopped fresh curly-leaf parsley

1. Place a large stockpot over high heat for 2 minutes. Add the canola oil, celery, carrot, onion, and potatoes and sauté until the vegetables are lightly browned, about 4 minutes. Remove the pot from the heat and, using a slotted spoon, transfer the vegetables to a bowl. Set aside.

2. Return the pot to high heat, add the cremini, shiitake, portobello, and oyster mushrooms, and cook, stirring, until browned, about 6 minutes. Be careful they do not burn. Add the garlic and

stir for 1 minute. Add the paprika, salt, pepper, and thyme and stir to combine. Pour in the wine and water, then stir in the sauerkraut. Bring the mixture to a boil, lower the heat to a gentle simmer, and cook uncovered, stirring occasionally, for 1 hour to blend the flavors.

3. Add the reserved vegetables and cook until the potatoes are tender, about 15 minutes. Ladle into individual bowls and serve immediately, garnished with the parsley.

CUCUMBER AND DILL SOUP
WITH PUMPERNICKEL CRUMBS
GURKENSUPPE

LONG BEFORE IT WAS TRENDY to make chilled or room-temperature soups out of every vegetable base imaginable, Germans were puréeing cucumbers to make this summertime specialty, which boasts plenty of cucumber flavor despite its simple starting point. The soup can be served at room temperature or covered and refrigerated for up to 2 days.

INGREDIENTS (SERVES 4 TO 6)

1 tbsp canola oil

1 yellow onion, diced

1 garlic clove, minced

2 English cucumbers, cut into ½-in/12-mm chunks

Grated zest and juice of 1 lemon

1 tbsp kosher salt

½ cup/25 g finely chopped fresh dill

½ cup/30 g finely chopped fresh curly-leaf parsley

Pumpernickel crumbs (see page 55) for garnish

½ cup/120 ml plain Greek yogurt

1. In a small frying pan, heat the canola oil over medium-high heat. Add the onion and garlic and cook, stirring occasionally, until translucent, about 4 minutes. Transfer the mixture to a bowl and let cool completely.

2. In a blender or the food processor, combine the cucumbers, cooled onion-garlic mixture, lemon zest and juice, and salt and process on medium speed until the mixture is perfectly smooth, about 3 minutes. Turn off the blender, add the dill and parsley, and then process for 1 minute longer.

3. Ladle the soup into individual bowls, top with the pumpernickel crumbs and a spoonful of yogurt, and serve.

TRUFFLED HAZELNUT AND POTATO SOUP

HASELNUSSSUPPE

THIS DISH, which Jeremy originally created as an hors d'oeuvre for a dinner at New York's James Beard House, is modern in approach but old-school as far as its ingredients. Hazelnuts are a frequent indulgence for Germans, used to make desserts, savory stuffings, spaetzle (made with hazelnut flour), and even schnapps. The velvety purée of this soup is made even more luxurious with garnishes of shaved truffle and crispy cracklings. We typically use duck skin cracklings for this dish, but store-bought pork rinds (*chicharrones*) will provide plenty of crunch and flavor.

INGREDIENTS (SERVES 4 TO 6)

2 tbsp unsalted butter

1 yellow onion, diced

2 russet potatoes, peeled and diced

2 cups/270 g blanched hazelnuts

4 cups/960 ml water

1 cup/240 ml heavy cream

1 tbsp sugar

1 tbsp kosher salt

2 tbsp black truffle oil

1 small fresh black truffle, or 1 tbsp canned or jarred black truffle peelings

One 6-oz/170-g package pork rinds

1. In a medium saucepan, melt the butter over medium heat. Add the onion and cook, stirring occasionally, until translucent, about 4 minutes. Add the potatoes and hazelnuts and cook, stirring, for 2 minutes. Add the water and cream, raise the heat to medium-high, and bring to a boil. Turn the heat to medium and simmer, uncovered, until the potatoes are tender, about 25 minutes. Add the sugar and salt and stir to combine.

2. Remove the saucepan from the heat and let cool slightly. Working in batches if necessary, transfer the mixture to a blender and process until smooth and creamy, about 6 minutes.

3. Return the soup to the saucepan and reheat gently until hot. Ladle into individual bowls and drizzle with the truffle oil, dividing it evenly. Using a truffle slicer or a V slicer, shave the black truffle evenly over the bowls, or divide the truffle peelings evenly among the bowls. Finish off each bowl with a scattering of the pork rinds (you will not need the entire package), breaking them up as you add them. Serve immediately.

ASPARAGUS AND RAMP SOUP
WITH SAUTÉED MORELS
BÄRLAUCH-SPARGEL-SUPPE

THIS SOUP, which pairs green and white asparagus with the forager's prized *Bärlauch* (ramps), presents ingredients in a way that is common in Germany but rare in the United States. (If you cannot find ramps, substitute 4 green onions, white and green parts, and 2 or 3 garlic cloves.) Morel mushrooms are the first choice here, as they have the best flavor to stand up to the asparagus and cream, but they are expensive and can be difficult to source. You can trade them out for nearly any other type of mushroom except for white mushrooms, which are too mildly flavored. If you substitute shiitake, oyster, or other mushrooms with caps larger than ½ in/12 mm, cut the mushrooms into ½-in/12-mm pieces.

INGREDIENTS (SERVES 4 TO 6)

1 lb/455 g white asparagus

1 lb/455 g green asparagus

2 tbsp canola oil

2 tbsp unsalted butter

1 yellow onion, diced

1 tbsp kosher salt

8 ramps, bulbs and leaves, finely minced

Leaves from 10 sprigs fresh thyme

1 cup/240 ml heavy cream

4 oz/115 g morel mushrooms, rinsed briefly in cool water, then brushed clean with a soft-bristled brush and ends trimmed

1 shallot, sliced

1 garlic clove, minced

1 tbsp sherry vinegar

1. Using a vegetable peeler, peel each asparagus spear from just below the tip to the base, removing the tough skin and capturing the peels in a medium saucepan. Snap off the woody base from each spear where it breaks easily and add the bottoms to the saucepan with the peels. Add water to cover to the saucepan and bring to a boil over high heat. Turn the heat to medium and simmer for 10 minutes. Strain the asparagus stock through a fine-mesh sieve into a container and discard the solids. You should have about 8 cups/1 L. Measure out 4 cups/960 ml for the soup and reserve the remainder for another use or discard.

2. Cut the asparagus into about 2-in/5-cm lengths. Rinse the saucepan, return it to medium heat, and add 1 tbsp each of the canola oil and butter. When the butter melts, add the onion and salt and cook, stirring occasionally, until the onion is translucent, about 4 minutes. Add the ramps, asparagus, leaves from 6 thyme sprigs, and the 4 cups/960 ml reserved stock. Raise the heat to high and bring to a boil. Turn the heat to medium and simmer, uncovered, until the asparagus is tender, 8 to 10 minutes. Add the cream and continue to cook for 2 minutes.

3. Remove the pan from the heat and let cool slightly. Working in batches if necessary, transfer the mixture to a blender and process on medium-high speed until smooth, about 2 minutes.

4. In a medium frying pan, combine the remaining canola oil and butter over high heat. When the butter has melted, add the mushrooms and cook, stirring frequently, until browned, about 6 minutes. Add the shallot and garlic and cook for another 3 minutes. Add the thyme leaves from the remaining 4 sprigs and the vinegar and stir to mix well. Remove from the heat.

5. Return the soup to the saucepan and reheat gently until hot. Ladle into individual bowls and top with the mushrooms, dividing them evenly. Serve immediately.

BEER AND CHEESE SOUP
BIERKÄSESUPPE

A FALL AND WINTER DISH that we've served at the restaurant for years, this soup always sells like crazy. With beer, Emmentaler cheese, and rye bread together in one warming, satisfying bowl, those steady sales are no surprise. It's important to use a malty dark lager, like Spaten Optimator, for this soup, as hoppier beers will turn it bitter. Accompany the soup with freshly baked bread or soft pretzels (see page 18).

INGREDIENTS (SERVES 6 TO 8)

2 tbsp unsalted butter

1 small yellow onion, diced

1 small leek, white and green parts, diced

2 garlic cloves, crushed

1 small carrot, peeled and diced

1 stalk celery, diced

Three 12-oz/340-ml bottles Spaten Optimator, Ayinger Celebrator, or other double-bock beer

1 lb/455 g Emmentaler or Gruyère cheese, grated

2 tbsp Worcestershire sauce

Leaves from 3 sprigs fresh thyme

1½ tbsp kosher salt

Freshly ground black pepper

2 slices hearty rye bread, cut into 1-in/2.5-cm pieces

2 tbsp chopped fresh chives

1. Heat a medium Dutch oven or stockpot over medium-high heat for 2 minutes. Add the butter, onion, leek, garlic, carrot, and celery and cook, stirring often, until the vegetables have softened and are lightly browned, about 6 minutes. Add the beer, cheese, Worcestershire, thyme, salt, and 1 tsp pepper and stir well. Bring to a boil, stirring often, then turn the heat to medium and simmer uncovered, stirring often, for 45 minutes to blend the flavors. Add the bread and continue cooking, stirring often, until the bread softens, about 15 minutes.

2. Remove the pan from the heat and let cool slightly. Working in batches, transfer to a blender and process on medium speed until completely smooth, about 2 minutes.

3. Return the soup to the pot and reheat gently until hot. Ladle into individual bowls, sprinkle with the chives and a dusting of pepper, if desired, and serve immediately.

CREAMY SAUERKRAUT AND WHEAT BEER SOUP

SAUERKRAUTSUPPE

JEREMY HOSTED A COLLABORATIVE DINNER with chef Josef Nagler of Schneider Weisses Brauhaus in Munich, and one of Nagler's dishes inspired this one. Everyone in the Brauhaus Schmitz kitchen thought a sauerkraut-based soup sounded weird, but it turned out excellent. Using potato and cream to build the base mellows out the sour notes of the kraut, as does the addition of Hefeweizen, which adds touches of sweetness and yeast.

INGREDIENTS (SERVES 4 TO 6)

2 tbsp unsalted butter

1 yellow onion, diced

1 garlic clove, minced

1 lb/455 g sauerkraut, homemade (see page 194) or store-bought, drained

2 tsp finely chopped fresh marjoram

1 cup/240 ml heavy cream

2 cups/480 ml wheat beer, preferably Hefeweizen

2 russet potatoes, peeled and diced

1. In a medium saucepan, melt the butter over medium-high heat. Add the onion and garlic and cook, stirring occasionally, until translucent, about 4 minutes. Add the sauerkraut and marjoram and stir to combine. Pour in the cream and beer, stir to combine, and bring to a boil. Turn the heat to medium, cover, and simmer for 20 minutes. Add the potatoes, re-cover, and cook until the potatoes are tender, about 25 minutes longer.

2. Remove the pan from the heat and let cool slightly. Working in batches if necessary, transfer the mixture to a blender and process on low speed until smooth and creamy, about 3 minutes.

3. Return the soup to the saucepan and reheat gently until hot. Ladle into individual bowls and serve immediately.

ENGLISH PEA SOUP
WITH SHRIMP AND FENNEL CONFIT
FRISCHE ERBSENSUPPE

GERMAN PEA SOUPS are more often made with yellow split peas than with their fresh green cousins, so this spin on pea soup results in a much brighter bowl. No cream is called for here. Instead, the fennel confit that tops each bowl delivers a wonderful richness, while the garnish of large shrimp adds both color and a delicious hint of the sea.

INGREDIENTS (SERVES 4 TO 6)

2 bulbs fennel, thinly sliced crosswise

1 cup/240 ml extra-virgin olive oil

1 tsp kosher salt, plus 1 tbsp

2 fresh bay leaves, or ½ dried bay leaf

Grated zest of 1 lemon

2 tbsp canola oil

1 leek, white and green parts, diced

1 cup/140 g fresh or frozen shelled English peas

2 cups/480 ml vegetable or chicken stock, low sodium if store-bought

½ tsp ground white pepper

12 large shrimp, peeled and deveined

1 tbsp finely chopped fresh mint

1. In a small saucepan, combine the fennel, olive oil, 1 tsp salt, bay leaves, and lemon zest over medium heat. When the oil is hot, turn the heat to low and cook the fennel slowly until tender, about 30 minutes. Remove from the heat and let cool to room temperature. (The fennel confit can be stored in an airtight container in the refrigerator for up to 1 week.)

2. In a medium saucepan, combine 1 tbsp of the canola oil and the leek over medium heat and cook, stirring occasionally, until the leek has softened, about 6 minutes. Add the peas, stock, remaining 1 tbsp salt, and white pepper; raise the heat to high; and bring to a boil. Turn the heat to medium and simmer until the peas are soft, about 10 minutes.

3. Just before the soup is ready, heat the remaining 1 tbsp canola oil in a medium frying pan over medium-high heat. When the oil is hot, add the shrimp and cook, turning as needed, until they are opaque throughout, 4 to 6 minutes. Using a slotted spoon, transfer the shrimp to a plate and cover to keep warm.

4. When the soup is ready, remove from the heat and let cool slightly. Add the mint and stir to mix well. Working in batches if necessary, transfer the soup to a blender and process on low speed until smooth, about 2 minutes.

5. Return the soup to the pan and reheat gently until hot. Ladle into individual bowls and garnish with the shrimp and fennel confit. Serve immediately.

DUCK, BARLEY, AND MUSHROOM SOUP

ENTENSUPPE

BEEF AND BARLEY are a classic German soup combination, but here the beef has been swapped out in favor of duck, giving this cool-weather dish a bolder personality. Start with a whole bird, using its meat for the soup and its carcass for the rich, beery duck broth backdrop. If you are feeling under the weather because of a winter cold, this soup will definitely put you on the road to recovery. It is chicken noodle soup, new German style.

INGREDIENTS (SERVES 6 TO 8)

STOCK

2 carrots, peeled and cut into 1-in/2.5-cm pieces

1 yellow onion, cut into 1-in/2.5-cm pieces

4 stalks celery, cut into 1-in/2.5-cm pieces

1 leek, white and green parts, cut into 1-in/2.5-cm pieces

One 5-to-6-lb/2.3-to-2.7-kg Long Island duck

4 fresh bay leaves, or 2 dried bay leaves

6 sprigs fresh thyme

2¼ cups/455 g pearl barley

1 yellow onion, diced

1 carrot, peeled and diced

2 stalks celery, diced

4 garlic cloves, minced

1 fresh bay leaf, or ½ dried bay leaf

1 lb/455 g wild (chanterelle or porcini) and/or cultivated (portobello, cremini, or shii-take) mushrooms, trimmed and cut into thin slices

4 cups/960 ml Spaten Optimator, Ayinger Celebrator, or other double-bock beer

2 tbsp finely chopped fresh curly-leaf parsley

1. *To make the broth,* preheat the oven to 375°F/190°C. Put the carrots, onion, celery, and leek in the center of a roasting pan, forming a vegetable "rack" for the duck. Place the duck, breast-side up, on top of the vegetables and place in the oven. Roast until an instant-read thermometer inserted into a leg away from bone registers 150°F/65°C, about 1½ hours.

2. Transfer the duck to a large plate and set aside to cool until it can be handled. Place the roasting pan on the stove top over two burners. Turn on the heat to medium and pour enough water into the pan to come about 1 in/2.5 cm up the sides. Using a wooden spoon or spatula, scrape the bottom of the pan to loosen any browned bits. When the water reaches a boil, remove the pan from the heat and strain the liquid through a fine-mesh sieve into a large stockpot. Discard the solids.

(Continued)

3. When the duck is cool enough to handle, pull the meat with the skin intact off the carcass. Shred the meat and skin into pieces, put into a bowl, cover, and set aside for adding to the soup. Break up the carcass into a few big pieces, add to the stockpot with the deglazed pan liquid, and then add water to cover, the bay leaves, and thyme. Place over medium-high heat, bring to a boil, turn the heat to medium, and simmer, uncovered, for about 1 hour.

4. Remove the stockpot from the heat, strain the broth through the fine-mesh sieve into a heatproof container, and discard the solids. You should have about 8 cups/2 L for the soup. (Reserve the remainder for another use.) Using a large metal spoon, skim off the fat from the surface. (Alternatively, let the broth cool, cover, and refrigerate the broth and the reserved duck meat separately overnight. The next day, skim off the solidified fat from surface of the broth and finish the soup.)

5. Rinse out the stockpot, pour the broth back into it, and bring to a boil over high heat. Add the barley, onion, carrot, celery, garlic, and bay leaf. Lower the heat to a simmer and cook, uncovered, for 30 minutes. Add the mushrooms, beer, and the reserved duck meat and continue to simmer until the barley is tender, about 15 minutes longer.

6. Ladle into individual bowls and garnish with the parsley. Serve immediately.

4

FISH, SHELLFISH & POULTRY

FISCH UND GEFLÜGEL

GERMAN CUISINE HAS NEVER BEEN CONSIDERED FISH HEAVY, especially in the eyes of the everyday schnitzel-loving American. But even though pork will likely always dominate the Teutonic protein discussion, fish and shellfish hold an important place in German regional cooking. In the south, freshwater rivers and lakes provide an abundance of versatile white-fleshed fish. Trout is the most common catch, but pike, perch, and even carp make appearances on dinner tables, too. On the opposite end of the country, where Germany dips into the North and Baltic Seas, eaters enjoy cod, salmon, mackerel, mussels, and clams, often prepared in a manner that share style points with Scandinavian fish cookery.

Contemporary aquaculture has spread high-quality fish and shellfish throughout the country. Nowadays, a fish shop in Munich has just as much access to fresh stock as one in due-north Hamburg, so that fewer fillets need to be pickled or otherwise preserved. The recipes in this chapter celebrate both geographical ends of German fish and shellfish cuisine. Be sure to become friendly with your local fishmonger to ensure access to the freshest catch.

Much the same can be said of poultry in German cooking. Chicken, duck, and goose are widely available and regularly prepared, but these birds have never earned the same fame that pork has. For this chapter, we sought out some atypical and, in some cases, archaic preparations to show appreciation for what Germans have been doing for centuries. Here, you'll find recipes for chicken brined in Riesling, as it is done in the Moselle River valley; our backyard barbecue spin on *Paprikash*, a classic of central Europe; and a new version of duck with pomegranate, a German cookbook staple in vogue in past decades.

PANFRIED MACKEREL
WITH PARSLEY-CAPER BROWN BUTTER
MAKRELLE

AS NOTED EARLIER, fresh herring has proven difficult to source in the United States, so in this dish, mackerel, which mimics the oily, up-front flavor of herring, has been substituted. This is a straight-ahead dish that's easy to make and is delicious. Panfrying and butter basting yield fillets that are wonderfully crispy (leave the skin on), and the brown butter, lemon, and capers complement them. If you or your dining companions are averse to fishiness, seek out Spanish mackerel, which is a little less funky by nature.

INGREDIENTS (SERVES 4)

4 skin-on mackerel fillets, 6 to 7 oz/170 to 200 g each

1 tbsp canola oil

1 tsp kosher salt

½ tsp freshly ground black pepper

2 tbsp unsalted butter

2 tbsp finely chopped fresh curly-leaf parsley

1 tbsp brine-cured capers, drained

1 tbsp hot smoked Spanish paprika

Juice of ½ lemon

1. Cut three diagonal slashes 1 in/2.5 cm long and ¼ in/6 mm deep on the skin side of each mackerel fillet. This prevents the fillets from curling during cooking. In a medium sauté pan, heat the canola oil over high heat. Place the fillets, skin-side down, in the pan and season the flesh side with the salt and pepper. Cook until the skin is browned and crispy, about 4 minutes. Using a spatula, carefully flip the fillets and cook for another 2 minutes. The flesh should be firm to the touch and have turned white. Using the spatula, transfer the fillets to a plate and cover to keep warm.

2. Drain off the oil from the pan and return the pan to medium heat. Add the butter and heat it until it starts to brown, about 2 minutes. Add the parsley, capers, and paprika and stir to combine. Remove from the heat and whisk in the lemon juice.

3. Arrange the fillets on a platter and pour the brown butter sauce over them. Serve immediately.

GRILLED SALMON
WITH HORSERADISH AND
PICKLED BEET SAUCE
LACHS

THE COMBINATION of pickled beets and horseradish is common in eastern Europe, and its popularity has been co-opted by German cooks, who have long used both elements in the kitchen. If possible, use homemade pickled beets to create the robustly flavored topping for this simple salmon dinner.

INGREDIENTS (SERVES 4)

1 cup/155 g sliced pickled beets, homemade (see page 189) or store-bought, roughly chopped

3 tbsp freshly grated horseradish or prepared horseradish

2 tbsp finely chopped fresh curly-leaf parsley

Grated zest and juice of 1 lemon

Canola oil for the grill rack

1 tsp coriander seeds

1 tsp dill seeds

1 tsp kosher salt

½ tsp freshly ground black pepper

4 skin-on salmon fillets, 6 to 8 oz/170 to 225 g each

1. In a food processor, combine the pickled beets, horseradish, parsley, and lemon zest and juice and pulse until the beets are coarsely chopped. Transfer to a small bowl and set aside.

2. Prepare a medium-hot fire in a charcoal or gas grill. Brush the grill rack with canola oil.

3. In a spice grinder, combine the coriander seeds and dill seeds and pulse until coarsely ground. Pour into a small bowl and stir in the salt and pepper. Evenly coat the skin side of each salmon fillet with one-fourth of the spice mixture.

4. Place the fillets, skin-side down, on the grill rack and cook until the skin starts to get crispy and the fillets can be easily lifted from the grill, 5 to 6 minutes. Flip the fillets and continue to cook until the flesh is firm to the touch and begins to flake when prodded with a knife tip, about 5 minutes longer.

5. Transfer the fillets to a platter and let rest for 5 minutes. Serve each fillet with one-fourth of the beet-horseradish mixture.

GRILLED WHOLE TROUT
STUFFED WITH HERBED BUTTER
FORELLE

A WHOLE FISH, filled like a pocketbook with simple ingredients and grilled over a live fire, is a common main meal in Germany's mountainous regions. Freshwater trout are most often sold whole, gutted and split with the head left on, making them perfect for stuffing with lemon slices that flavor the flesh from the inside out. The herbed butter here then bastes the fish from both the inside and the outside.

INGREDIENTS (SERVES 2)

HERBED BUTTER

8 oz/225 g unsalted butter, at room temperature

2 tbsp finely chopped fresh curly-leaf parsley

2 tbsp finely chopped fresh dill

2 tbsp finely chopped fresh chives

Leaves from 4 sprigs fresh thyme

Grated zest and juice of 1 lemon

Canola oil for the grill rack

2 whole trout, cleaned and butterflied with head intact

1 lemon, cut into 6 slices ½ in/12 mm thick

Kosher salt and freshly ground black pepper (optional)

1. *To make the herbed butter,* in a food processor or a blender, combine the butter, parsley, dill, chives, thyme, and lemon zest and juice and process or beat until thoroughly mixed.

2. Lay a sheet of waxed paper on a work surface. Scoop the butter mixture onto the paper, spreading it in a lengthwise strip on the sheet and leaving about 1 in/2.5 cm uncovered on each end. Roll the paper around the butter, pressing against the paper lightly to shape the butter into a long, even cylinder. Grasp the ends and twist in opposite directions to seal closed. Refrigerate the butter for up to 2 weeks. (You will need only about 6 tbsp/85 g of the butter for this recipe. Use the remainder on top of grilled steaks, chops, or fish.)

3. Prepare a medium-hot fire in a charcoal or gas grill. Brush the grill rack with canola oil.

4. Line up 3 lemon slices in the cavity of each trout, then stuff each cavity with about 2 tbsp of the butter.

5. Place the trout on the grill rack and grill, turning once, about 4 minutes on each side. Check the fish to see if they are done; the flesh should be moist, firm, and just turning white.

6. Transfer the trout to a platter or individual plates and top with more herbed butter, using about 1 tbsp on each fish. Season with salt and pepper, if desired. Serve immediately.

COD-STUFFED CABBAGE ROLLS
WITH DILL CREAM SAUCE
FISCHROULADEN

THE CLASSIC NORTHERN GERMAN PAIRING of cabbage with fish gets a literal twist here: we are treating the duo nontraditionally, wrapping a seasoned cod cake in cabbage leaves, baking the parcels, and then topping them with a mustard-and-cream-thickened pan sauce brightened by fresh dill. This recipe was the result of a day when a line cook accidentally chopped an entire night's worth of cod into bite-size pieces that was supposed to remain whole. We had to do something with it, so we came up with this idea as a special and got some great feedback.

INGREDIENTS (SERVES 6)

1 head Savoy cabbage

1½ lb/600 g cod fillets

1 tbsp canola oil

1 yellow onion, chopped

1 garlic clove, minced

1 cup/80 g fine dried bread crumbs

1 egg, lightly beaten

2 tbsp finely chopped fresh curly-leaf parsley

2 tbsp finely chopped fresh dill

Kosher salt and freshly ground white pepper

4 tbsp/60 ml mild German mustard

2 cups/480 ml dry white wine

1 cup/240 ml heavy cream

1. Fill a large pot half full with water and bring to a boil over high heat. Immerse the cabbage in the boiling water and cook until the outer leaves have loosened and can be peeled off, about 5 minutes. To test, using a wire skimmer, carefully lift out the cabbage head and try to peel away the outer leaves; if they do not come away, return the head to the water for a couple minutes more, then test again. Peel off as many whole leaves as you can easily remove without tearing them. Return the cabbage head to the boiling water and repeat the process until you have six whole leaves. Arrange the leaves, interior-side up, in a single layer on a work surface and let cool completely. Reserve the remaining cabbage for another use.

2. Preheat the oven to 350°F/180°C.

3. Finely chop the cod fillets, discarding any errant bones. Put the fish in a medium bowl, cover, and refrigerate until ready to use.

4. In a medium sauté pan, heat the canola oil over medium-high heat. Add the onion and garlic and cook, stirring occasionally, until the onion is translucent, about 4 minutes. Remove from the heat and let cool completely.

(Continued)

5. Add the cooled onion mixture, bread crumbs, egg, parsley, dill, 1 tsp salt, ½ tsp white pepper, and 2 tbsp of the mustard to the cod and mix well.

6. Divide the cod mixture into six equal portions and shape each portion into a rough log shape. Put a portion about 1 in/2.5 cm from the bottom edge of a cabbage leaf, where the stem is the thickest. Lift the edge of the leaf over the filling and then roll up the filling in the leaf, folding in the sides as you roll. Place the roll, seam-side down, in a baking dish just large enough to accommodate all the rolls. Repeat with the remaining cabbage leaves and filling portions. Pour the wine into the dish.

7. Bake the rolls until a thermometer inserted into the center of a roll registers 145°F/63°C. Remove the dish from the oven, pour off the liquid into a medium saucepan, and cover the rolls in the dish to keep them warm.

8. Place the saucepan over medium-high heat and bring the liquid to a boil. Whisk in the cream until heated through and lightly thickened, then whisk in the remaining 2 tbsp mustard. Season with salt and white pepper.

9. Arrange the cabbage rolls on a platter and pour the sauce over the top. Serve immediately.

SEAFOOD STEW WITH PAPRIKA BROTH

FISCHGULASCH

THIS IS ESSENTIALLY THE BOUILLABAISSE OF NORTHERN GERMANY, and it's eaten in a manner very similar to that of the French seafood stew: in a bowl with a spoon and plenty of crusty bread for sopping up the delicious broth. Although you will need to assemble a number of ingredients, the dish itself goes together quickly and easily. A mixture of hot and sweet Hungarian paprika gives the broth its memorable flavor and rich color.

INGREDIENTS (SERVES 6 TO 8)

1 tbsp canola oil

1 leek, white and green parts, cut into slices 1 in/2.5 cm thick

1 carrot, cut into slices 1 in/2.5 cm thick

4 garlic cloves, minced

3 tbsp sweet Hungarian paprika

1 tsp hot Hungarian paprika

2 cups/480 ml dry white wine

4½ cups/1 L fish stock or water

1½ tbsp Maggi seasoning sauce

Grated zest and juice of 2 lemons

2 Yukon gold potatoes, cut into 1-in/2.5-cm cubes

1 lb/455 g skin-on or skin-less cod fillets, cut into 1-in/2.5-cm pieces

1 lb/455 g mussels, scrubbed and debearded

20 clams, scrubbed

16 shrimp, peeled and deveined

Leaves from 6 sprigs fresh thyme

2 tbsp finely chopped fresh curly-leaf parsley

Crusty sourdough bread for serving

1. In a large stockpot, combine the canola oil, leek, and carrot over medium-high heat and cook, stirring often; until lightly browned, about 6 minutes. Add the garlic and the sweet and hot paprikas and stir to combine. Add the wine, stock, Maggi sauce, and lemon zest and juice. Stir to combine, raise the heat to high, and bring to a boil. Add the potatoes, turn the heat to medium, and simmer for 15 minutes. Add the cod and continue to simmer for 5 minutes. Add the mussels and clams, discarding any that fail to close to the touch, and then add the shrimp and thyme. Cook until the clams and mussels open and the shrimp are opaque, about 6 minutes.

2. Ladle the stew into shallow individual bowls, discarding any clams or mussels that failed to open. Garnish with the parsley and serve immediately, accompanied with the bread.

CHICKEN CUTLETS
STUFFED WITH WHITE ASPARAGUS, SPINACH, AND PARMESAN CHEESE
HÜHNERROULADEN

THIS DISH is most commonly prepared with beef slices *(Rinderrouladen)*, which are rolled around pickles, mustard, bacon, and onions, simmered in a heavy stock, and then served with gravy. Here, the same concept is lightened considerably with chicken, white asparagus, and spinach. Spicy mustard heightens the flavor of the mustard cream sauce that is spooned over the rolls. Serve with semolina egg noodles (see page 163), spaetzle (see page 168), or *Schupfnudeln* (see page 174).

INGREDIENTS (SERVES 6)

18 white asparagus spears

Kosher salt

1 tbsp canola oil

1 tbsp unsalted butter

1 yellow onion, diced

1 garlic clove, minced

Freshly ground black pepper

1 cup/55 g roughly chopped spinach

½ cup/55 g grated Parmesan cheese

6 boneless, skinless chicken breasts or chicken cutlets

2 cups/480 ml chicken stock, low sodium if store-bought

2 cups/480 ml dry white wine

1 cup/240 ml heavy cream

1½ tbsp Löwensenf or Dijon spicy mustard

1 tbsp finely chopped fresh curly-leaf parsley

1. Preheat the oven to 350°F/180°C.

2. Using a vegetable peeler, peel each asparagus spear from just below the tip to the base, removing the tough skin. Snap off the woody base from each spear where it breaks easily and then even the ends with a paring knife.

3. Fill a medium saucepan two-thirds full with water, bring to a boil over high heat, and season with salt. It should not be too salty; instead, it should be seasoned just enough to resemble a good chicken stock. While the water is heating, ready an ice-water bath in a large bowl and line a plate with paper towels. Place both near the stove.

4. Plunge the asparagus into the boiling water and cook until almost tender, about 6 minutes; the timing depends on the size of the asparagus. Using a wire skimmer or tongs, transfer the asparagus to the ice-water bath, immersing the spears completely. Leave them in the ice bath until chilled, about 5 minutes. Remove the spears from the ice bath and drain on the towel-lined plate.

5. In a medium sauté pan, heat the canola oil and butter over medium-high heat. Add the onion and garlic, season with a little salt and pepper, and cook, stirring occasionally, until the onion is translucent, about 4 minutes. Add the spinach and cook until wilted, about 3 minutes. Using a slotted spoon, transfer the contents of the pan to a medium bowl and let cool completely. Once the mixture is cool, add the cheese and mix well.

6. If using chicken breasts, place a breast on a cutting board and top with a sheet of plastic wrap. Using a meat mallet, and starting at the thickest part of the breast, gently pound the breast, working from the center to the edge, until the meat is an even ½ in/12 mm thick. Repeat with the remaining breasts, then line up the breasts on a work surface. If you have purchased chicken cutlets, they should already be the correct thickness; line them up on the work surface.

7. Spread the spinach mixture evenly over the chicken pieces. Cut each asparagus spear in half crosswise, so the pieces will fit crosswise on the chicken pieces. Place six asparagus pieces on top of the spinach mixture on a piece of chicken and roll up the chicken around the filling. Place the roll, seam-side down, in a baking dish just large enough to accommodate all of the rolls. Form five more rolls the same way and add to the dish.

8. Pour the stock, wine, and cream into the bottom of the baking dish. Place the dish in the oven and bake for 30 minutes. To test for doneness, insert an instant-read thermometer into the center of a roll; it should register 160°F/71°C.

9. Remove the dish from the oven, pour off the liquid into a medium saucepan, and cover the rolls in the dish to keep them warm.

10. Place the saucepan over medium-high heat and bring the liquid to a boil. Cook until reduced by half, about 15 minutes. Whisk in the mustard and parsley.

11. Arrange the rolls on a platter and pour the sauce over the top. Serve immediately.

GRILLED MARINATED CHICKEN WITH PAPRIKA

PAPRIKASH

PAPRIKASH, which has its origins in Hungary, is a popular eastern European export that has been adopted by German cooks. In the traditional recipe—admittedly, every household has its own version—chicken is braised in stock with onions and paprika and the resulting sauce is finished with sour cream. Here, the creamy sauce, with hints of citrus and heat, has been transformed into a marinade, and the flavors bloom on the grill. You can use boneless chicken breasts for this recipe, but skin-on half chickens allow you to include both white and dark meat in the mix. This is a favorite meal of the Brauhaus Schmitz staff. It is also a great outdoor summertime recipe for the grill. Accompany the chicken with Potato and Cucumber Salad with Dill Vinaigrette (page 65), a perfect seasonal side dish.

INGREDIENTS (SERVES 2)

1 large or 2 small shallots, sliced

2 garlic cloves, sliced

Juice of 1 lemon

1 tbsp kosher salt

¼ tsp freshly ground black pepper

2 tbsp sweet Hungarian paprika

½ tsp hot Hungarian paprika

2 tbsp plain yogurt

2 half chickens, about 1¾ lb/800 g each

Canola oil for the grill rack

1. In a small bowl, combine the shallot, garlic, lemon juice, salt, pepper, sweet and hot paprikas, and yogurt and mix well. Rub the half chickens with the yogurt mixture on all sides, place them in a container, cover, and refrigerate for at least 24 hours, or up to 2 days.

2. Prepare a medium fire in a charcoal or gas grill. Brush the grill rack with canola oil.

3. Place the half chickens, skin-side down, on the grill rack and cook for about 20 minutes, making sure the skin doesn't burn. Turn the chicken over and continue to cook until an instant-read thermometer inserted into a thigh away from bone registers 160°F/71°C, about 20 minutes longer.

4. Transfer the chicken to individual plates and serve immediately.

SPAETZLE WITH CHICKEN, CHANTERELLES, AND CREAM
JÄGERSPÄTZLE

HERE, THE ELEMENTS OF *RAHMSCHNITZEL*, meat cutlets in an ample cream sauce, have been reimagined into a substantial main course that features chicken. If you have the time, make the spaetzle at home; if not, purchase dried spaetzle and your supper will be ready in just minutes. Chanterelles are an elegant mushroom to use in this dish, but oyster or *maitake* (hen-of-the-woods) mushrooms would also work well. *Halbtrocken* (half-dry) Riesling has a slight touch of sweetness; a similar white wine can be substituted.

INGREDIENTS (SERVES 6 TO 8)

1 tbsp unsalted butter

1 tbsp canola oil, plus more for oiling the bowl

1 lb/455 g boneless, skinless chicken breasts or thighs

Kosher salt and freshly ground black pepper

8 oz/225 g chanterelle mushrooms, trimmed

1 yellow onion, thinly sliced

3 garlic cloves, minced

½ tsp finely chopped fresh thyme

1 tsp finely chopped fresh rosemary

1 cup/240 ml halbtrocken Riesling

½ cup/120 ml crème fraîche

1 recipe Buckwheat Spaeztle (page 168), or 1 lb/455 g dried spaetzle, cooked

2 tbsp finely chopped fresh curly-leaf parsley

1. In a large sauté pan, heat the butter and canola oil over medium-high heat. Season the chicken with 1 tsp salt and ½ tsp pepper, add the chicken to the pan, and cook, turning once, until opaque throughout, 5 to 6 minutes on each side. Transfer the chicken to a plate and keep warm.

2. Turn the heat to medium, add the mushrooms to the pan, and cook, stirring occasionally, until browned, about 5 minutes. Season the mushrooms with salt and pepper and add the onion, garlic, thyme, and rosemary. Cook, stirring occasionally, until the onion is translucent, about 2 minutes. Add the wine, raise the heat to high, bring to a steady simmer, and cook until the liquid is reduced by half, about 4 minutes. Add the crème fraîche and spaetzle and stir to combine until heated through.

3. Cut the chicken into slices about ½ in/12 mm thick and add them to the pan along with the parsley. Stir to mix evenly and heat through, then transfer to a serving dish and serve immediately.

CHICKEN BRAISED IN RIESLING

HUHN IN RIESLING SOSSE

WE HAVE ALREADY DEDICATED PLENTY OF SPACE to Germany's obsession with beer, so it is only correct that we turn our attention to wine. For this balanced main dish, which pays homage to the wine-producing regions along the Moselle and Rhine Rivers, we braise our bird in Riesling (use something nice, but don't break the bank) and include seedless grapes to add some texture and sweetness. The finishing touch of crème fraîche is a nod to adjacent Alsace. Since this is a light dish, you can get away with serving the chicken and sauce over spaetzle (see page 168), egg noodles (see page 163), small dumplings of any type, or mashed potatoes.

INGREDIENTS (SERVES 4)

2 tbsp canola oil

1 tbsp unsalted butter

1 chicken, about 4 lb/1.8 kg, quartered, or 4 boneless, skinless chicken breasts or thighs

Kosher salt and freshly ground black pepper

1 yellow onion, sliced

1 leek, white and green parts, sliced

2 garlic cloves, minced

1 bunch seedless green grapes, picked off the stem

4 cups/960 ml dry Riesling

2 cups/480 ml chicken stock, low sodium if store-bought

Leaves from 1 bunch fresh tarragon

1 cup/240 ml crème fraîche or sour cream

1. Preheat the oven to 350°F/180°C.

2. In a large Dutch oven, heat the canola oil and butter over medium-high heat. Season the chicken with salt and pepper and, working in batches if necessary to avoid crowding, add the chicken to the pot. Cook, turning once, until the chicken is golden brown on both sides, about 4 minutes on each side. Using a slotted spoon or tongs, transfer the chicken to a plate and reserve.

3. With the pot still over medium-high heat, add the onion, leek, and garlic and cook, stirring often, until translucent, about 4 minutes. Add half of the grapes and cook, stirring occasionally, for 3 minutes. Return the chicken to the pot and pour in the Riesling and stock. Cover, place the pot in the oven, and cook for 30 minutes. To check for doneness, insert an instant-read thermometer into the thickest part of the chicken (away from bone if using quartered chicken); it should register 160°F/71°C.

4. Remove the pot from the oven. Using a slotted spoon, transfer the chicken to a deep platter. Place the pot over medium heat, add the tarragon, crème fraîche, and the remaining grapes, and stir to combine and heat through. Pour the sauce over the chicken and serve immediately.

PILSNER-AND-PICKLE-JUICE-BRINED
ROASTED CHICKEN
HENDL

RUNNING A RESTAURANT that goes through an unbelievable number of pickles puts us in a predictable, well, pickle. We have huge amounts of leftover pickle juice that we don't know what to do with. It seemed like such a waste to throw it away, so we began to experiment with it as a brine for meats. Our most successful effort was this chicken, which also relies on beer to tenderize and flavor the flesh. The bird must sit in the brine for at least one full day, but two full days are best. It might be a challenge for you to come up with enough pickle juice to submerge a whole chicken. For a shortcut that produces a similar result, make up the pickling liquid for Pickled Mixed Vegetables on page 190.

INGREDIENTS (SERVES 4 GENEROUSLY)

4 cups/960 ml pilsner

4 cups/960 ml dill pickle juice

1 tbsp kosher salt

1 tbsp sugar

6 garlic cloves, crushed

One 5-lb/2.3-kg whole chicken

1. In a large stockpot, combine the pilsner, pickle juice, salt, sugar, and garlic and bring to a boil over high heat. Remove from the heat and let cool completely, then cover and refrigerate until cold.

2. Submerge the chicken in the brine; top the bird with a heavy plate or other weight if necessary to keep it submerged in the liquid. Re-cover the pot and refrigerate for at least 24 hours, or preferably 48 hours.

3. Preheat the oven to 425°F/220°C.

4. Remove the chicken from the brine and pat dry. Place the chicken, breast-side up, on a rack in a roasting pan. Pour a small amount of water (about ¼ in/6 mm deep) into bottom of the pan. Roast the chicken until an instant-read thermometer inserted into a thigh away from bone registers 160°F/71°C, 1 to 1½ hours.

5. Remove the chicken from the oven, transfer it to a platter or cutting board, tent loosely with aluminum foil, and let rest for about 10 minutes before carving and serving.

DUCK LEGS WITH ROASTED VEGETABLES

ENTENKEULE

IF YOU BROWSE through old German cookbooks, you will discover the seemingly non-Germanic combination of pomegranate seeds and duck. That led to the development of this pomegranate juice–based jus for duck legs, the sweetness of which has been tempered by the addition of salty Maggi seasoning sauce. The legs roast over a bed of root vegetables.

INGREDIENTS (SERVES 6)

6 duck legs

2 turnips, peeled and cut into 1-in/2.5-cm cubes

2 carrots, peeled and cut into 1-in/2.5-cm cubes

2 parsnips, peeled and cut into 1-in/2.5-cm cubes

2 Yukon gold potatoes, cut into 1-in/2.5-cm cubes

1 yellow onion, cut into 1-in/2.5-cm cubes

4 sprigs fresh tarragon

Kosher salt and freshly ground black pepper

POMEGRANATE JUS

One 16-oz/480-ml bottle pomegranate juice

2 tbsp Maggi seasoning sauce

¼ tsp ground allspice

1 tbsp red wine vinegar

Juice of 2 oranges

1 tbsp peeled and finely minced fresh ginger

1. Preheat the oven to 400°F/200°C.

2. Heat a small roasting pan on the stove top over medium-high heat. Add the duck legs, skin-side down, and cook until the skin turns golden brown, about 6 minutes. Turn the duck legs over and cook for another 5 minutes. Remove the pan from the heat.

3. Using a slotted spoon, transfer the duck legs to a plate. Add the turnips, carrots, parsnips, potatoes, and onion to the same pan and stir to mix. Place the tarragon sprigs on top of the vegetables and season with salt and pepper. Place the duck legs, skin-side up, on the vegetables and transfer the pan to the oven.

4. Roast the duck legs and vegetables, turning the vegetables occasionally, until an instant-read thermometer inserted into the thickest part of a leg away from bone registers 165°F/74°C, about 1 hour.

5. *To make the pomegranate jus,* in a small saucepan, combine the pomegranate juice, Maggi sauce, allspice, vinegar, orange juice, and ginger over high heat and bring to a boil. Turn the heat to medium and cook until reduced by half, about 20 minutes.

6. Transfer the duck legs and vegetables to a platter and pour the warm jus over the top. Serve immediately.

ROASTED GOOSE
WITH PRETZEL-APPLE STUFFING AND GEWÜRZTRAMINER GLAZE
GANS

ALTHOUGH IT IS AN OLD-FASHIONED HOLIDAY DISH in America, a whole roasted goose is the most common contemporary choice for a German Christmas dinner. This is a variation on that German tradition, with apple and ginger offering wintry sustenance in the form of a bright pretzel-based stuffing. Juniper, another holiday mainstay, plays an important role in this preparation. It is always best to err on the conservative side when using juniper berries, however, as the flavor can be quite strong—a fact that anyone who is put off by dry gin will attest to.

INGREDIENTS (SERVES 8 GENEROUSLY)

STUFFING

3 cups/185 g cut-up day-old soft pretzels (½-in/12-mm chunks), homemade (see page 18) or store-bought

½ cup/115 g unsalted butter

2 cups/250 g diced Granny Smith apples

1 yellow onion, diced

3 stalks celery, diced

1½ cups/360 ml chicken stock, low sodium if store-bought

2 tbsp finely minced fresh sage, or 2 tsp dried sage

2 tbsp finely chopped fresh marjoram

1½ tbsp peeled and finely minced fresh ginger

1 tbsp kosher salt

½ tsp freshly ground black pepper

One 10- to 12-lb/4.5- to 5.4-kg whole goose

GLAZE

2 cups/480 ml Gewürztraminer or other sweet white wine

1 cup/240 ml chicken stock, low sodium if store-bought

1 tbsp juniper berries

¼ cup/55 g firmly packed dark brown sugar

2 fresh bay leaves, or 1 dried bay leaf

1 tsp kosher salt

1. *To make the stuffing,* put the pretzel pieces in a large bowl. In a large sauté pan, melt the butter over medium-high heat. Add the apples, onion, and celery and cook, stirring occasionally, until the mixture is a light golden brown, about 15 minutes. Add the stock, sage, marjoram, ginger, salt, and pepper and stir to combine, then continue cooking for 2 minutes. Remove the pan from the heat and pour the contents over the pretzel pieces. Mix all of the ingredients together until they are evenly distributed and the mixture is sticky. Let the stuffing cool to room temperature.

2. Preheat the oven to 375°F/190°C.

(Continued)

3. Remove the giblets and neck from the goose, if included, and reserve for another use. Spoon the stuffing into the body cavity (no need to skewer, sew, or tie closed) and place the bird, breast-side up, in a roasting pan. Pour water to a depth of about 1½ in/4 cm into the bottom of the pan.

4. Place the bird in the oven and roast until an instant-read thermometer inserted into the thigh away from bone registers 165°F/74°C, 3 to 3½ hours.

5. *To make the glaze,* in a small saucepan, combine the Gewürztraminer, stock, juniper berries, brown sugar, bay leaves, and salt over medium-high heat and bring to a boil, stirring to dissolve the sugar. Cook until reduced by half, about 20 minutes.

6. When the bird is ready, transfer it to a platter or cutting board, tent loosely with aluminum foil, and let rest for 10 minutes. Spoon the stuffing out of the cavity and carve the bird. Drizzle the glaze over the bird and the stuffing and serve immediately.

5

MEAT & GAME

FLEISCH UND
WILDFLEISCH

THE PIG, IN ALL ITS WONDROUS FORMS, is the animal that dominates mainstream German cooking, and if you ran your eyes over the daily purveyor order forms for Brauhaus Schmitz, you would see that the food we make respects that dominance, especially when it comes to our house-made sausages. But we also make sure to emphasize many of the other traditions that inform German meat mania.

Germany boasts a vibrant hunting tradition, especially in the Black Forest and mountainous Bavarian regions, so game is a revered component of the national meat culture. Because Jeremy grew up in Reading, Pennsylvania, the seat of Berks County, a hunter's paradise, game has always had a place on our menu. Beef does not carry the same importance in Germany as it does in the States—steaks as thick as a phone book are a favorite of many Americans—but it has its place and is growing in popularity.

About one-fourth of the recipes in this chapter are regional, dishes that are just as unfamiliar to a German who grew up a couple hours away from their origin as they are to an American who knows only schnitzel. You will also find in these pages the tradition of doing things slow and low: marinating and then braising over gentle heat for hours or sometimes even days. Finally, this chapter will fill you in on spit roasting, grilling, smoking, and more, plus it will provide new ideas on how to lighten some of the heavier German fare.

SMOKED PORK AND BACON SAUSAGE

SPECKWURST

ALL OF THE SAUSAGES WE MAKE at Brauhaus Schmitz involve a roughly three-to-one ratio of pork meat to pork fat. For this recipe, we replace the fat portion with smoked bacon, grind it up, and then smoke it a *second* time when we smoke the sausages to amp up the flavor. The result is a highly versatile wurst that can be eaten hot or cold, grilled at a tailgate party, or even incorporated into a meat stuffing. For the bacon, forget store-bought presliced stuff and find a butcher who can provide you with true slab bacon, the smokier the better.

NOTE: *We measure the seasonings in this recipe in grams because of the need for precision when seasoning any sausage mixture. For the best results, use a digital scale.*

INGREDIENTS (MAKES 5 LB/2.3 KG OF SAUSAGE)

3 lb/1.4 kg boneless pork shoulder, cut into 1-in/2.5-cm cubes, or ground pork

2 lb/910 g slab bacon, cut into 1-in/2.5-cm cubes

40 g kosher salt

6 g pink curing salt #1

7 g freshly ground black pepper

5 g ground coriander

3 g ground ginger

3 g freshly grated nutmeg

3 g ground mace

About 3 ft/1 m hog casings, preferably 29 to 32 mm in diameter (optional)

1. Place the cubed pork, cubed bacon, and the meat grinder parts in the freezer until the pork and bacon are very cold and firm and the grinder parts are cold, about 1 hour. If using ground pork, you can skip putting it in the freezer.

2. In a small bowl, combine the kosher salt, curing salt, pepper, coriander, ginger, nutmeg, and mace and stir to mix thoroughly.

3. *If you are using pork shoulder,* set up the meat grinder according to the manufacturer's instructions and fit it with the medium grinding plate. Grind the pork and bacon into a large bowl. Add the seasoning mixture to the pork and bacon and mix well with your hands. Once the meat is seasoned, pass the meat through the grinder again.

If you are using ground pork, set up the meat grinder according to the manufacturer's instructions and fit it with the medium grinding plate. Grind the bacon into a large bowl and add the ground pork. Add the seasoning mixture to the pork and bacon and mix well with your hands. Once the meat is seasoned, pass the meat through the grinder again.

4. Cover the bowl and refrigerate the mixture while you set up the sausage stuffer. Or, if you prefer to make patties rather than stuff casings, shape the mixture into patties now, making them each about 3 in/7.5 cm in diameter and ½ in/12 mm thick. The patties can be cooked right away on a grill or on the stove top, or you can arrange them on a sheet pan, stacking them separated by squares of waxed paper, cover, and refrigerate.

5. Soak the casings in lukewarm water to cover for 30 minutes, then run cool water through them to rinse away some of the salt. Set up the sausage stuffer according to the manufacturer's instructions, attaching the proper-size stuffing tube for the casing. Slide a casing onto the stuffing tube, tie a knot at the end of it, and begin stuffing the casing, making sure it is not filled too tightly or it will burst during cooking.

6. When all of the sausage mixture is in casings, starting at the tied end of a stuffed casing, measure about 6 in/15 cm for the first sausage and pinch at that point to mark the length. Then measure off the second sausage length and pinch again. Now, twist the first pinched point a few times in one direction. Measure the third link, pinch it, and then twist it a few times in the same direction as the first link. Measure the fourth link, pinch the point, and then measure the fifth link, pinch it, and twist a few times in the same direction as before. Continue in this way, twisting only every other link, until you reach the end of the casing, then tie off the end.

7. Coil the sausages on a sheet pan and refrigerate, uncovered, overnight to dry slightly.

8. The next day, set up your smoker according to the manufacturer's instructions and heat to 180°F/82°C. Uncoil the sausages and hang them from sticks or arrange them on racks in the smoker, spacing them at least 1 in/2.5 cm apart to ensure the smoke can circulate freely. Smoke the sausages for 1½ hours. To test if the sausages are ready, insert an instant-read thermometer into the center of a sausage; it should register 155°F/68°C.

9. Remove the sausages from the smoker and immediately plunge them into an ice-water bath until well chilled (this ice-water dunk keeps the sausages from shriveling or shrinking). Remove the sausages from the ice bath, pat dry, cover, and refrigerate overnight.

10. You can cut between the links and cook the sausages on a grill or in a 300°F/150°C oven until heated through. They can also be wrapped tightly in plastic wrap and refrigerated for up to 3 days, or frozen for up to 2 months.

FOIE GRAS LIVERWURST
STOPFLEBERWURST

JEREMY HAS BEEN MAKING LIVERWURST FOREVER, beginning when he cooked with his dad, who learned the traditional way to prepare it from an old German butcher in Reading. Years later, Jeremy was asked to participate in a citywide Foie Gras Friday promotion, and combined that technique with fancy duck liver to create a treat that hits both the high and low end. Liverwurst, typically made with calf or pork liver, is peasant food, something that's always been looked down on when compared with more refined offal preparations like French pâté. At Brauhaus Schmitz, we up its status for our diners by slipping some foie gras into the typically humble wurst. Serve it spread on Golden Flaxseed Mixed Bread (page 25) or Sourdough Barley Bread with Sage Topping (page 22) for Brotzeit.

NOTE: *In this recipe, unlike the other sausage recipes, you need to measure only the kosher salt and curing salt in grams. For the best results, use a digital scale.*

INGREDIENTS (MAKES ABOUT 5 LB/2.3 KG OF SAUSAGE)

1½ lb/680 g boneless pork shoulder, cut into 1-in/2.5-cm cubes	40 g kosher salt	1½ tsp ground cardamom
	8 g pink curing salt #1	8 oz/225 g crushed ice
4 fresh bay leaves, or 2 dried bay leaves	1½ tsp dried sage	1½ lb/680 g fresh foie gras, trimmed of blood spots and veins, cut into 1-in/2.5-cm cubes, and partially frozen
1 lb/455 g chicken or duck livers	1½ tsp dried marjoram	
	1 tsp ground ginger	
8 oz/225 g yellow onion, diced	2½ tsp ground white pepper	About 2 ft/61 cm beef middle casings, 2½ in/ 6 cm in diameter
	2½ tsp ground allspice	
	1½ tsp ground coriander	

1. Fill a large pot two-thirds full with water and bring to a boil over high heat. Turn the heat to a simmer, add the pork and bay leaves, and cook for 1½ hours. Using a slotted spoon, transfer the pork cubes to a plate lined with paper towels. Discard the liquid.

2. Set up the meat grinder according to the manufacturer's instructions and fit it with the medium grinding plate. Grind the warm pork cubes, chicken livers, and onion into a large bowl. Pass the mixture through the grinder again.

3. Unless you have a very large food processor, you will need to grind this in two or three batches. In the food processor, combine the ground meat mixture, kosher salt, curing salt, sage, marjoram, ginger, white pepper, allspice, coriander, cardamom, and ice. Start the food processor and process the mixture until smooth. Add the foie gras and continue to process until smooth and emulsified, about 4 minutes.

4. Soak the casings in lukewarm water to cover for 30 minutes, then run cool water through them to rinse away some of the salt. Set up the sausage stuffer according to the manufacturer's instructions, attaching the proper-size stuffing tube for the casing. Slide a casing onto the stuffing tube, tie a knot at the end of it, stuff 8 in/20 cm of the casing, tie again, and then cut the casing 1 in/2.5 cm after the tie to remove the link. Repeat filling the casings until you have used up all of the stuffing. As each link is finished, place it in a pot large enough to hold all of the sausages.

5. When all of the links are in the pot, cover with cold water, place the pot on the stove top, turn the heat to medium-high, and bring to a simmer. Turn the heat to medium and keep just below a simmer so the sausages don't burst. Cook the sausages until an instant-read thermometer inserted into the center of a sausage registers 155°F/68°C, about 30 minutes. Meanwhile, prepare an ice-water bath in a large container.

6. When the sausages are ready, transfer them to the ice-water bath and let stand for 10 minutes to cool thoroughly. Remove the sausages from the ice water, pat dry, place in a covered container, and refrigerate overnight before serving. The sausages will keep refrigerated for up to 10 days. Or, they can be wrapped tightly in plastic wrap and frozen for up to 2 months.

SPICY HUNGARIAN-STYLE BRATWURST

UNGARISCHE BRATWURST

WHEN PEOPLE COMPLAIN that there's no spicy food in Germany, we like to serve them a link of this traditional smoked sausage. To be fair, *Ungarische* brats are Austro-Hungarian in origin, but they've long been embraced and adapted by German cooks. The unmistakable red color of this sausage comes from the generous mix of hot and sweet paprikas, the key to its big, brash flavor. If you do not have a smoker, these sausages are still tasty treated as fresh sausages.

NOTE: *We measure the seasonings in this recipe in grams because of the need for precision when seasoning any sausage mixture. For the best results, use a digital scale.*

INGREDIENTS (MAKES 5 LB/2.3 KG OF SAUSAGE)

5 lb/2.3 kg boneless pork shoulder, cut into 1-in/2.5-cm cubes, or ground pork

40 g kosher salt

25 g sweet Hungarian paprika

24 g hot smoked Spanish paprika

6 g freshly ground black pepper

5 g caraway seeds

5 g red pepper flakes

4 g pink curing salt #1

5 garlic cloves, minced

About 3 ft/1 m hog casings, preferably 29 to 32 mm in diameter (optional)

1. Place the cubed pork and the meat grinder parts in the freezer until the pork is very cold and firm and the grinder parts are cold, about 1 hour. If using ground pork, skip this step.

2. In a bowl, combine the kosher salt, sweet and hot paprikas, black pepper, caraway seeds, red pepper flakes, curing salt, and garlic and stir to mix thoroughly.

3. *If you are using pork shoulder,* set up the meat grinder according to the manufacturer's instructions and fit it with the medium grinding plate. Grind the pork into a large bowl. Add the seasoning mixture to the pork and mix well with your hands. Once it is seasoned, pass the meat through the grinder again.

If you are using ground pork, put it in a large bowl. Add the seasoning mixture to the pork and mix well with your hands.

4. Cover the bowl and refrigerate the mixture while you set up the sausage stuffer. Or, if you prefer to make patties rather than stuff casings, shape the mixture into patties now, making them each about 3 in/7.5 cm in diameter and ½ in/12 mm thick. The patties can be cooked right away on a grill or on the stove top. Or you can arrange them on a sheet pan, stacking them separated by squares of waxed paper, cover, and refrigerate.

5. Soak the casings in lukewarm water to cover for 30 minutes, then run cool water through them to rinse away some of the salt. Set up the sausage stuffer according to the manufacturer's instructions, attaching the proper-size stuffing tube for the casing. Slide a casing onto the stuffing tube, tie a knot at the end of it, and begin stuffing the casing, making sure it is not filled too tightly or it will burst during cooking.

6. When all of the sausage mixture is in casings, starting at the tied end of a stuffed casing, measure about 6 in/15 cm for the first sausage and pinch at that point to mark the length. Then measure off the second sausage length and pinch again. Now, twist the first pinched point a few times in one direction. Measure the third link, pinch it, and then twist it a few times in the same direction as the first link. Measure the fourth link, pinch the point, and then measure the fifth link, pinch it, and twist a few times in the same direction as before. Continue in this way, twisting only every other link, until you reach the end of the casing, then tie off the end.

7. *If you are not smoking the sausages*, coil them on a sheet pan, cover, and refrigerate overnight to rest. (They need to rest or the casing will come apart when you cut between the sausages.)

If you are smoking the sausages, coil them on a sheet pan and refrigerate, uncovered, overnight to dry slightly.

8. The next day, set up your smoker according to the manufacturer's instructions and heat to 180°F/82°C. Uncoil the sausages and hang them from sticks or arrange them on racks in the smoker, spacing them at least 1 in/2.5 cm apart to ensure the smoke can circulate freely. Smoke the sausages for 1½ hours. To test if the sausages are ready, insert an instant-read thermometer into the center of a sausage; it should register 155°F/68°C.

9. Remove the sausages from the smoker and immediately plunge them into an ice-water bath until well chilled (this ice-water dunk keeps the sausages from shriveling or shrinking). Remove the sausages from the ice bath, pat dry, cover, and refrigerate overnight.

10. You can cut between the links and cook the sausages on a grill or in a 300°F/150°C oven until heated through. They can also be wrapped tightly in plastic wrap and refrigerated for up to 3 days, or frozen for up to 2 months.

NUREMBERG-STYLE BRATWURST

BRATWURST

LONG BEFORE Brauhaus Schmitz opened, Jeremy, having discovered that all of the commercial brats were underseasoned, developed a bratwurst recipe. Lack of seasoning is definitely not the case with these brats, and based on their reception at the restaurant, our customers agree. We go through more than 100 lb/45 kg of these sausages each week, sold by the half and full meter, plus they won a Best of Philly award from *Philadelphia* magazine in 2012. Using fresh marjoram here provides a punch that you won't find in supermarket sausage.

NOTE: *We measure the seasonings in this recipe in grams because of the need for precision when seasoning any sausage mixture. For the best results, use a digital scale.*

INGREDIENTS (MAKES 5 LB/2.3 KG OF SAUSAGE)

5 lb/2.3 kg boneless pork shoulder, cut into 1-in/ 2.5-cm cubes, or ground pork

40 g kosher salt

7 g ground white pepper

3 g caraway seeds

3 g ground mace

3 g ground ginger

12 g finely chopped fresh marjoram

About 3 ft/1 m hog casings, preferably 29 to 32 mm in diameter (optional)

1. Place the cubed pork and the meat grinder parts in the freezer until the pork is very cold and firm and the grinder parts are cold, about 1 hour. If using ground pork, skip this step.

2. In a bowl, combine the salt, white pepper, caraway seeds, mace, ginger, and marjoram and stir to mix thoroughly.

3. *If you are using pork shoulder,* set up the meat grinder according to the manufacturer's instructions and fit it with the medium grinding plate. Grind the pork into a large bowl. Add the seasoning mixture to the pork and mix well with your hands. Once it is seasoned, pass the meat through the grinder again.

If you are using ground pork, put it in a large bowl. Add the seasoning mixture to the pork and mix well with your hands.

4. Cover the bowl and refrigerate the mixture while you set up the sausage stuffer. Or, if you prefer to make patties rather than stuff casings, shape the mixture into patties now, making them each about 3 in/7.5 cm in diameter and ½ in/12 mm thick. The patties can be cooked right away on a grill or on the stove top. Or you can arrange them on a sheet pan, stacking them separated by squares of waxed paper, cover, and refrigerate.

(Continued)

5. Soak the casings in lukewarm water to cover for 30 minutes, then run cool water through them to rinse away some of the salt. Set up the sausage stuffer according to the manufacturer's instructions, attaching the proper-size stuffing tube for the casing. Slide a casing onto the stuffing tube, tie a knot at the end of it, and begin stuffing the casing, making sure it is not filled too tightly or it will burst during cooking.

6. When all of the sausage mixture is in casings, starting at the tied end of a stuffed casing, measure about 6 in/15 cm for the first sausage and pinch at that point to mark the length. Then measure off the second sausage length and pinch again. Now, twist the first pinched point a few times in one direction. Measure the third link, pinch it, and then twist it a few times in one direction as the first link.

Measure the fourth link, pinch the point, and then measure the fifth link, pinch it, and twist a few times in the same direction as before. Continue in this way, twisting only every other link, until you reach the end of the casing, then tie off the end.

7. Coil the sausages on a sheet pan, cover, and refrigerate overnight to rest. (They need to rest or the casing will come apart when you cut between the sausages.)

8. You can cut between the links and cook the sausages on a grill or in a 300°F/150°C oven until heated through. They can also be wrapped tightly in plastic wrap and refrigerated for up to 2 days, or frozen for up to 2 months.

GRILLED TRI-TIP
WITH CHERRY TOMATO RELISH
TAFELSPITZ

JEREMY'S FATHER is from the Central Coast of California, where tri-tip, a grill-friendly boneless roast cut from the bottom sirloin (outer hip) of a cow, is the cornerstone of Santa Maria–style barbecue. The same cut is common in Bavarian and Austrian cooking, where it is boiled and served with freshly grated horseradish, a dish known as *Tafelspitz*. Because we could not bring ourselves to boil such a beautiful roast, we have taken this popular German cut and treated it to a classic California preparation.

INGREDIENTS (SERVES 6 TO 8)

Canola oil for the grill rack

One 1½-lb/680-g tri-tip

1 tbsp kosher salt

1 tsp freshly ground black pepper

RELISH

½ pt/340 g cherry tomatoes, quartered through the stem end

2 tsp sherry vinegar

1 tbsp finely chopped fresh tarragon

2 green onions, white and green parts, sliced

1 shallot, thinly sliced

½ tsp kosher salt

1 tbsp honey

2 tbsp extra-virgin olive oil

1. Prepare a medium-hot fire in a charcoal or gas grill. Brush the grill rack with canola oil.

2. Sprinkle all sides of the roast with the salt and pepper and place it on the grill directly over the fire. Cook until well browned on the first side, about 10 minutes. Rotate the roast a quarter turn and brown on the next side, about 10 minutes. Repeat to brown the remaining sides the same way, adjusting the timing as needed. Move the roast to a cooler area on the grill rack and close the lid. Cook until an instant-read thermometer inserted into the center of the roast registers 130°F/55°C for medium-rare, about 1 hour.

3. *To make the relish,* in a small bowl, combine the cherry tomatoes, vinegar, tarragon, green onions, shallot, salt, honey, and olive oil and stir until well combined. Let rest for about 30 minutes, stirring occasionally, before serving.

4. When the roast is done, transfer it to a cutting board, tent loosely with aluminum foil, and let rest for 10 minutes. Carve the roast into slices ½ in/12 mm thick and arrange the slices on a platter. Top with the relish and serve immediately.

BRISKET BRAISED IN BEER
BIERFLEISCH

AS MENTIONED PREVIOUSLY, at Brauhaus Schmitz, we like to cook with beer as much as possible, and this dish is another good example of how we incorporate beer into our recipes. (Of course, we all like to drink it, too.) Although brisket is not a widely eaten cut in Germany, it does make appearances. It is the perfect cut for braising, especially in a dark lager that's malty, sweet, and not too hoppy. This is a hearty, filling dish ideal for fall and winter.

INGREDIENTS (SERVES 6 TO 8)

1 tbsp canola oil

1 tbsp unsalted butter

1 beef brisket, 5 to 6 lb/ 2.3 to 2.7 kg

Kosher salt and freshly ground black pepper

1 yellow onion, sliced

2 tbsp all-purpose flour

2 cups/480 ml beef stock, low sodium if store-bought

2 cups/480 ml Spaten Optimator, Ayinger Celebrator, or other double-bock beer

4 garlic cloves, minced

4 fresh bay leaves, or 2 dried bay leaves

Leaves from 4 sprigs fresh thyme

1 tbsp Maggi seasoning sauce

1. Preheat the oven to 325°F/165°C.

2. In a Dutch oven, heat the canola oil and butter over medium-high heat. Season the brisket on all sides with salt and pepper and, when the fat is hot, place the brisket in the pot. Cook until well browned on the first side, about 10 minutes. Turn the brisket over and cook until well browned on the second side, about 10 minutes. Transfer the brisket to a plate and set aside.

3. Add the onion to the pot and cook over medium-high heat, stirring often, until lightly browned, about 10 minutes. Sprinkle the flour over the onion and stir to combine, then scrape up any bits that may have stuck to the bottom. Pour in the stock and beer, add the garlic, bay leaves, thyme, Maggi sauce, and 1 tsp pepper and whisk thoroughly. Return the brisket to the pot and bring the liquid to a boil.

4. Remove the pot from the heat, cover, and transfer to the oven. Cook until the brisket is very tender when pierced with a fork, about 2½ hours.

5. Remove the pot from the oven, uncover, transfer the brisket to a plate, and cover to keep warm. Place the pot on the stove top over medium-high heat, bring to a boil, and cook until the sauce has thickened slightly, about 15 minutes. Remove and discard the bay leaves.

6. Transfer the brisket to a cutting board and cut into slices against the grain. Arrange the slices on a platter and pour the sauce over the top. Serve immediately.

SPIT-ROASTED BEEF
MARINATED IN ONION, GARLIC, PAPRIKA, AND HERBS
SPIESSBRATEN

THE STORY goes that *Spiessbraten*, the signature dish of the Rhineland city of Idar-Oberstein, arrived in Germany via gem miners who went to South America for work and brought live-fire "gaucho" cooking back home with them. Pork loin, butterflied and stuffed with herbs and seasonings, is the most common choice there, but the natural texture of flank steak also works well with this cooking technique. The rolled and stuffed meat is traditionally spit roasted, as the name implies, so if you have a spit attachment for your grill, go ahead and use it. Here, it is cooked on a grill rack to make the recipe accessible to more cooks. The finished dish will have a little kick to it, so consider serving it with a cooling side, such as Potato and Cucumber Salad with Dill Vinaigrette (page 65).

INGREDIENTS (SERVES 6 TO 8)

1¾ lb/800 g flank steak

1 yellow onion, sliced

1 bunch green onions, white and green parts, sliced

4 garlic cloves, minced

1 tbsp sweet Hungarian paprika

1 tsp hot smoked Spanish paprika

1 tsp dried marjoram

1 tbsp red wine vinegar

Kosher salt and freshly ground black pepper

2 tbsp grapeseed or canola oil, plus more for the grill rack

1. First, butterfly the flank steak. Place the steak on a cutting board, with a narrow end facing you. Using a long, thin-bladed knife, cut through the steak horizontally, stopping ½ in/12 mm from the opposite edge. Open the steak flat like a book. Using a meat mallet, gently and evenly pound the steak so that it is an even thickness at all points.

2. In a small bowl, combine the yellow onion, green onions, garlic, sweet and hot paprikas, marjoram, vinegar, 2 tsp salt, 1 tsp pepper, and the grapeseed oil and mix well. Spread this mixture evenly over the flank steak.

3. Then, starting from a long side, roll up like a jelly roll. Using kitchen string, tie the roll at 2-in/5-cm intervals, to ensure it holds together during grilling. Place the roll in an airtight container and refrigerate overnight.

4. The next day, prepare a medium-hot fire in a charcoal or gas grill. Brush the grill rack with grapeseed oil.

(Continued)

5. Liberally sprinkle the entire outside of the rolled steak with salt and pepper and place it on the grill directly over the fire. Cook until well browned on the first side, about 4 minutes. Rotate the roll a quarter turn and brown on the next side, about 4 minutes. Repeat to brown the remaining two sides the same, adjusting the timing as needed. Move the roll to a cooler area on the grill rack and close the lid. Cook until an instant-read thermometer inserted into the center of the roll registers 130°F/55°C for medium-rare, about 1 hour.

6. Transfer the roll to a cutting board, tent loosely with aluminum foil, and let rest for 10 minutes. Cut the roll into slices ½ in/12 mm thick, arrange on a platter, and serve immediately.

BEEF AND VEAL MEATBALLS
WITH LEMON-CAPER CREAM SAUCE
KÖNIGSBERGER KLOPSE

HOW OLD-SCHOOL IS THIS DISH? Königsberg, the town these zesty balls are named after, doesn't even exist anymore. (Sandwiched between Poland and Lithuania, the city, now called Kaliningrad, has long been under Russian control.) Although the meatballs do combine beef and veal, it's the addition of a lemon and caper cream sauce that distinguishes them from the Mediterranean-style meatballs most of us are used to. Serve with mashed potatoes or spaetzle (see page 168).

INGREDIENTS (MAKES 16 MEATBALLS, SERVES 5 OR 6)

MEATBALLS

½ cup/115 g unsalted butter

1 yellow onion diced

2 garlic cloves, minced

8 oz/225 g ground beef

8 oz/225 g ground veal or pork

1 cup/80 g panko bread crumbs

1 tbsp finely chopped fresh marjoram

1 tbsp finely chopped fresh curly-leaf parsley

Grated zest and juice of ½ lemon

4 anchovy fillets, finely minced

½ tsp ground allspice

1 tbsp kosher salt

½ tsp freshly ground black pepper

SAUCE

1 tbsp unsalted butter

2 tbsp all-purpose flour

2 cups/480 ml chicken stock, low sodium if store-bought

1 cup/240 ml heavy cream

Juice of ½ lemon

1 tbsp brine-cured capers, drained

1 tbsp finely chopped fresh curly-leaf parsley

1. *To make the meatballs,* in a small sauté pan, melt 4 tbsp/55 g of the butter over medium heat. Add the onion and garlic, and cook, stirring occasionally, until the onion is translucent, about 4 minutes. Remove the pan from the heat.

2. In a small bowl, mix together the beef and veal. Add the bread crumbs, onion-garlic mixture, marjoram, parsley, lemon zest and juice, anchovy fillets, allspice, salt, and pepper and mix with your hands or a small handheld mixer until

thoroughly combined. Roll the meatball mixture into balls the size of a golf ball. You should have 16 balls. Set them aside on a sheet pan.

3. Line a large plate with paper towels. In a medium Dutch oven, melt the remaining butter over medium heat. Working in batches to avoid crowding, cook the meatballs until browned on all sides, about 8 minutes. Using a slotted spoon, transfer the meatballs to the towel-lined plate.

4. *To make the sauce,* drain off the fat from the Dutch oven and return the pot to medium heat. Add the butter and swirl it around to coat the bottom of the pan. Sprinkle in the flour and whisk until combined, scraping up any browned bits from the bottom. Pour in the stock, cream, and lemon juice. Whisk until thoroughly combined and bring the sauce to a simmer.

5. Return the meatballs to the Dutch oven and simmer until they are cooked through, 15 to 20 minutes.

6. Add the capers and parsley, stir to combine, and transfer to a serving dish. Serve immediately.

VEAL SWEETBREAD SCHNITZEL,
HOLSTEINER-STYLE
KALBSBRIES SCHNITZEL

WE SELL LOADS OF SCHNITZEL at Brauhaus Schmitz. Our guests choose among pork, veal, and chicken dressed in one of three styles. They are all big sellers, but the popularity of these plates always left us wanting to do something a little different. We nailed it with sweetbreads—so good prepared in any style, but hard not to love when battered, fried, and served new-school Holsteiner style, topped with a sauce of eggs, capers, and anchovies.

INGREDIENTS (SERVES 4 TO 6)

SWEETBREADS

2 whole veal sweetbreads, 10 to 12 oz/280 to 340 g each

1 tbsp kosher salt

1 cup/140 g all-purpose flour

3 eggs

1 cup/80 g panko bread crumbs, finely ground in a food processor

SAUCE

6 anchovy fillets, finely chopped

2 tbsp brine-cured capers, drained and finely chopped

2 hard-boiled eggs, peeled and finely chopped

½ bunch fresh curly-leaf parsley, chopped

1 tbsp white wine vinegar

1 tsp spicy mustard, homemade (see page 197) or store-bought (such as Löwensenf or Dijon)

1 tsp freshly ground black pepper

2 tbsp grapeseed or canola oil

Canola oil for frying

1. *To prepare the sweetbreads,* immerse them in a large bowl of cold water, cover, and refrigerate for about 12 hours, changing the water at least twice.

2. Drain the sweetbreads, place in a large saucepan, add water to cover and the salt, and bring to a boil over high heat. While the water is heating, ready an ice-water bath in a large bowl. When the water begins to boil, turn the heat to low and cook for 3 minutes. Using a wire skimmer, transfer the sweetbreads to the ice-water bath and let stand until completely cold, about 45 minutes.

3. Remove the sweetbreads from the water bath. Using your fingers and a paring knife, peel off the thin, clear membrane from the sweetbreads and cut away any bloody spots. Cut the sweetbreads crosswise into slices ½ in/12 mm thick. Lay the slices on a cutting board, cover them with plastic wrap, and gently pound them with a meat mallet until they are thin but still retain their shape.

4. Have ready a large plate. Put the flour in a medium bowl. In a second medium bowl, beat the eggs until blended. Put the bread crumbs in a third medium bowl. Pass the sweetbread slices, one at a time, through each bowl: dredge evenly in flour, shaking off the excess; coat with egg, allowing the excess to drip off; and finally, coat with crumbs, again shaking off the excess. As each slice is breaded, set it on the plate. When all of the slices are coated, cover and refrigerate until ready to cook.

5. *To make the sauce,* in a medium bowl, combine the anchovies, capers, eggs, parsley, vinegar, mustard, and pepper and stir to mix well. Whisk in the grapeseed oil until thoroughly combined. Set aside.

6. Pour the canola oil to a depth of about 1 in/ 2.5 cm into a deep cast-iron or other heavy frying pan and heat over medium heat to 300°F/150°C. (If you don't have a thermometer, drop a pinch of bread crumbs into the oil. If the crumbs sizzle immediately, the oil is ready.) Line a large heat-proof plate with paper towels.

7. Working in small batches to avoid crowding, carefully add the sweetbread slices, one at a time, to the hot oil and fry, turning once, until golden brown on both sides, 3 to 4 minutes on each side. Using a slotted spoon, transfer the slices to the towel-lined plate to drain and place in a warm oven. Repeat with the remaining sweetbread slices.

8. Arrange the sweetbread slices on a platter, top with the sauce, and serve immediately.

BONE-IN PORK CHOP SCHNITZEL
WITH PARSLEY SALAD

SCHWEINEKOTELETT "SCHNITZEL WIENER ART"

THIS IS OUR VARIATION ON CLASSIC *WIENER-ART* (VIENNA-STYLE) SCHNITZEL, using a bone-in pork chop pounded thinly, then panfried until crisp as if it is a traditional boneless cutlet. The bone adds plenty of flavor and also helps retain moisture in the meat. We've tweaked the recipe a little more with the topper, taking the traditionally separate garnishes of lemon and parsley and combining them into a salad.

INGREDIENTS (SERVES 4)

SALAD

1 cup/60 g roughly chopped fresh curly-leaf parsley

¼ cup/40 g roughly chopped cornichons

2 tbsp fresh lemon juice

3 tbsp grapeseed oil

Kosher salt and freshly ground black pepper

Four 12-oz/340-g bone-in pork loin chops

1 cup/140 g all-purpose flour

1 tsp dried marjoram

½ tsp sweet Hungarian paprika

1 tsp kosher salt

3 eggs

1½ cups/120 g panko bread crumbs

Vegetable oil for frying

1. *To make the salad,* in a small bowl, combine the parsley, cornichons, lemon juice, and grapeseed oil and stir well. Season with salt and pepper. Set aside.

2. Place a loin chop on a cutting board, cover with plastic wrap, and gently pound with a meat mallet until it is thin but still retains its shape. Repeat with the remaining chops.

3. Have ready a large plate. Put the flour in a medium bowl; add the marjoram, paprika, and salt; and stir to mix well. In a second medium bowl, beat the eggs until blended. Put the bread crumbs in a third medium bowl. Pass the chops, one at a time, through each bowl: dredge evenly in flour, shaking off the excess; coat with egg, allowing the excess to drip off; and finally, coat with crumbs, again shaking off the excess. As each chop is breaded, set it on the plate. When all of the chops are breaded, cover and refrigerate until ready to cook.

(Continued)

4. Pour the vegetable oil to a depth of about 1 in/2.5 cm into a deep cast-iron or other heavy frying pan and heat over medium heat to 300°F/150°C. (If you don't have a thermometer, drop a pinch of bread crumbs into the oil. If the crumbs sizzle immediately, the oil is ready.) Line a large heatproof plate or sheet pan with paper towels.

5. Working in batches to avoiding crowding, carefully add the chops, one at a time, to the hot oil and fry, turning once, until golden brown on both sides, 3 to 4 minutes on each side. Using tongs or a slotted spatula, transfer the chops to the towel-lined plate to drain and place in a warm oven. Repeat with the remaining chops.

6. Arrange the chops on a platter, top with the parsley salad, and serve immediately.

PORK SIRLOIN STEAK,
BREWMASTER STYLE
BRAUMEISTER SCHWEINESTEAK

IF YOU'RE LOOKING FOR A SUMMERTIME GRILLING ALTERNATIVE to burgers and franks, this is a good choice: a pork sirloin steak, with a satisfying and effortless beer-based marinade. The term *Braumeister* here refers to the marinade, which includes big flavors like mustard and garlic in addition to the robust dark beer. Serve the steaks with Heirloom Tomato Salad with Tarragon Vinaigrette and Goat Cheese (page 64) or Kohlrabi Salad with Black Garlic–Sour Cream Dressing (page 54).

INGREDIENTS (SERVES 6)

1 tsp caraway seeds

1 tbsp yellow mustard seeds

1 tsp kosher salt

1 tbsp sweet Hungarian paprika

1 tsp freshly ground black pepper

3 garlic cloves, minced

2 tsp finely chopped fresh marjoram, or 1 tsp dried marjoram

½ cup/120 ml Spaten Opti-mator, Ayinger Celebrator, or other double-bock beer

1 tbsp grapeseed oil

1 tsp Maggi seasoning sauce

1 tsp red wine vinegar

Six 8-oz/225-g bone-in pork sirloin steaks

Canola oil for the grill rack

1. In a spice grinder, combine the caraway seeds and mustard seeds and pulse until coarsely ground. Pour into a small bowl and stir in the salt, paprika, and black pepper. Add the garlic, marjoram, beer, grapeseed oil, Maggi sauce, and vinegar and whisk together until well combined.

2. Place the pork steaks in a shallow bowl and pour the spice mixture over the top. Turn the steaks to coat evenly, cover, and refrigerate overnight.

3. The next day, prepare a medium-hot fire in a charcoal or gas grill. Brush the grill rack with canola oil.

4. Place the steaks on the grill rack and cook, turning once, until nicely etched with grill marks on both sides and an instant-read thermometer inserted into the center of a steak away from the bone registers 150°F/65°C.

5. Transfer the steaks to a platter or individual plates and serve immediately.

SPICY MARINATED PORK SKEWERS
WITH PEPPERS, ONIONS, AND ZUCCHINI
SCHASCHLIK

GRILLED SKEWERS OF SPICY MARINATED MEAT are popular in many regions and countries, from eastern Europe to Russia to Iran to Mongolia. The style of *Schaschlik* eaten in Gemany originated in the Balkans and, over the years, the flavor-packed kebabs have become a common street food throughout the country. The marinade, with its crushed tomatoes and tomato juice, lemon, and mustard, has high acidity that breaks down the pork and allows the dry spices to work their flavor into the meat.

INGREDIENTS (SERVES 6 TO 8)

One 28-oz/780-g can crushed tomatoes

6 garlic cloves, minced

1 yellow onion, diced

1 stalk celery, diced

1 tbsp finely chopped curly-leaf parsley

2 tbsp spicy mustard, homemade (see page 197) or store-bought (such as Löwensenf or Dijon)

Juice of 1 lemon

2 tbsp honey

1 cup/240 ml tomato juice

1½ tbsp curry powder

1 tbsp kosher salt

1 tsp ground coriander

1 tsp celery seeds

5 lb/2.3 kg boneless pork shoulder, cut into 2-in/5-cm cubes

Canola oil for the grill rack

12 fresh or jarred cherry peppers

2 red onions, cut into 1-in/2.5-cm chunks

2 zucchini, cut into 1-in/2.5-cm chunks

1. In a blender, combine the tomatoes, garlic, yellow onion, celery, parsley, mustard, lemon juice, honey, tomato juice, curry powder, salt, coriander, and celery seeds and purée until smooth.

2. Put the pork cubes in a large bowl, pour in the purée, and toss and stir to coat the meat evenly. Cover and refrigerate overnight.

3. The next day, preheat the oven to 375°F/190°C.

4. Transfer the pork with its marinade to a baking dish, spreading the pork cubes in a single layer. Cover the dish, place in the oven, and cook the pork until the meat is tender and almost falling apart when prodded with a fork, about 2½ hours. Remove from the oven, let cool, cover, and refrigerate overnight until well chilled. (The pork is chilled so that it will slide easily onto skewers without breaking apart.)

5. Prepare a medium-hot fire in a charcoal or gas grill. Brush the grill rack with canola oil. Metal or wooden skewers may be used. If using wooden skewers, soak them in water to cover for about 30 minutes before loading them.

6. Thread the pork cubes onto the skewers, alternating them with the peppers, red onions, and zucchini. Place the skewers on the grill rack and cook, turning as needed, until the pork and vegetables are nicely etched with grill marks on all sides and are heated through, about 12 minutes total.

7. Transfer the skewers to a platter and serve immediately.

ROASTED RACK OF PORK
WITH APPLE CIDER SAUCE
SCHWEINSBRATEN

ROASTED PORK has long been an everyday German dish, and this recipe plays with and slightly refines that tradition. We start with a full pork rack for two reasons: it makes a beautiful presentation, and the bones make it easy to slice off big fat chops for everyone to enjoy. The cider sauce, made by reducing the liquid from the roasting pan, is a new yet simple take on the classic pork-and-apples combination.

INGREDIENTS (SERVES 8)

1 tsp caraway seeds

1 tbsp dry mustard, preferably Colman's

Kosher salt and freshly ground black pepper

1 tsp sweet Hungarian paprika

½ tsp ground ginger

2 tbsp honey

1 tbsp canola oil

1 tsp red wine vinegar

1 rack of pork, 4 to 5 lb/ 1.8 to 2.3 kg

1 carrot, peeled and cut into 1-in/2.5-cm chunks

1 yellow onion, cut into 1-in/2.5-cm chunks

2 stalks celery, cut into 1-in/2.5-cm pieces

8 garlic cloves

4 sprigs fresh thyme

Two 12-oz/360-ml bottles hard cider

1. In a small bowl, combine the caraway seeds, mustard, 1 tbsp salt, 1 tsp black pepper, paprika, ginger, honey, canola oil, and vinegar and stir to combine. Rub the mixture evenly over the rack of pork. Put the pork in a container, cover, and refrigerate overnight.

2. Preheat the oven to 350°F/180°C.

3. Mix together the carrot, onion, celery, garlic, and thyme in the center of a large roasting pan, forming a vegetable "rack" for the pork. Pour in the cider, then place the rack of pork, fat-side up, on the vegetables.

4. Transfer the pan to the oven and roast until an instant-read thermometer inserted into the rack away from bone registers 150°F/65°C, about 1½ hours.

5. Remove the pan from the oven and transfer the pork to a cutting board. Tent loosely with aluminum foil and let rest while you finish the sauce.

6. Strain the contents of the roasting pan through a fine-mesh sieve into a small saucepan and discard the solids. Place the saucepan over medium-high heat, bring to a boil, and boil until reduced by half, about 20 minutes. Remove from the heat, season with salt and pepper, and keep warm.

7. Carve the rack of pork between the bones and arrange the chops on a platter. Top with the cider sauce and serve immediately.

ROASTED LAMB SHOULDER
WITH GREEN HERB SAUCE
LAMMBRATEN IN GRÜNER SOSSE

YOU'RE NOT GOING TO SEE MUCH LAMB IN GERMANY. Along with beef, it's always been overshadowed by the almighty pig, but this recipe is our way of nodding to lamb preparations in the plains of northern Germany, where it is sometimes served as a Sunday roast. Carve out some time for this recipe, as you'll get the best results if you slowly cook the marinated shoulder. At the restaurant, we chill the finished roast, slice it, and crisp the pieces in a hot pan before serving. But if you are cooking at home, it's better to eat it right away. The sauce, based on a trio of distinctive herbs—sorrel, tarragon, watercress—is a Hessian take on pesto; here, we substitute spinach for the sorrel. Serve with panfried potatoes.

INGREDIENTS (SERVES 6 TO 8)

8 garlic cloves, minced

2 tbsp spicy mustard, homemade (see page 197) or store-bought (such as Löwensenf or Dijon)

½ bunch fresh curly-leaf parsley, chopped

1 tbsp white wine vinegar

2 tbsp grapeseed or canola oil, plus more for frying

2 tsp kosher salt

1 tsp freshly ground black pepper

1 boneless lamb shoulder roast, about 4½ lb/2 kg

1 carrot, peeled and cut into slices 1 in/2.5 cm thick

4 stalks celery, cut into slices 1 in/2.5 cm thick

1 large yellow onion, cut into 1-in/2.5-cm chunks

SAUCE

2 tbsp chopped fresh curly-leaf parsley

2 tbsp chopped fresh chives

2 tbsp chopped fresh tarragon

1 cup/40 g chopped watercress

1 cup/55 g chopped spinach

1 shallot, chopped

1½ tbsp spicy mustard, homemade (see page 197) or store-bought (such as Löwensenf or Dijon)

2 tbsp white wine vinegar

1 tbsp kosher salt

1 tsp ground white pepper

4 hard-boiled eggs, peeled and chopped

1. In a bowl, combine the garlic, mustard, parsley, vinegar, grapeseed oil, salt, and pepper and mix well. Rub the mixture evenly over the lamb shoulder. Place the lamb in a container, cover with plastic wrap, and refrigerate for at least 24 hours, or up to 2 days.

2. Preheat the oven to 375°F/190°C.

3. Mix together the carrot, celery, and onion in the center of a roasting pan, forming a vegetable "rack" for the lamb. Add just enough water to the pan to reach the top of the vegetables. Place the lamb shoulder on the "rack" of vegetables.

(Continued)

4. Transfer the pan to the oven and roast until an instant-read thermometer inserted into the thickest part of the roast registers 165°F/73°C and the meat is very tender, about 3½ hours.

5. Remove the pan from the oven, transfer the lamb to a platter, let cool, cover, and refrigerate overnight. (Chilling the lamb overnight ensures that it can be neatly sliced for frying.) Pour the pan juice through a fine-mesh sieve into a heatproof container, let cool, cover, and refrigerate overnight.

6. *To make the sauce,* the next day in a food processor, combine the parsley, chives, tarragon, watercress, spinach, and shallot and process until smooth, about 2 minutes. Add the mustard, vinegar, salt, and white pepper and process until thoroughly combined. Transfer to a bowl and stir in the eggs. (Or, if you prefer, reserve the eggs as a garnish.)

7. Remove the lamb from the refrigerator and cut against the grain into slices 1 in/2.5 cm thick. Place a large sauté pan over medium-high heat and coat the bottom lightly with oil. When the pan is hot, working in batches, add the slices to the pan and cook, turning once, until browned on both sides, about 3 minutes on each side. The slices should have a nice crust on both sides. Transfer the slices to a heatproof platter and keep them warm in a low oven. Repeat with the remaining slices, adding more oil to the pan as needed. Meanwhile, scoop the fat off of the reserved pan juices, then reheat the juices in a small saucepan over low heat until hot.

8. When all of the slices are browned, spoon the hot pan juices over the slices, then top with the sauce. If you have reserved the eggs as a garnish, sprinkle them over the top. Serve immediately.

VENISON MEDALLIONS
WITH JUNIPER–BLACK PEPPER BRANDY SAUCE
REHMEDAILLONS

GERMANY BOASTS SO MANY HUNTERS that venison is used in many different forms: sausages, salamis, roasts, chops, steaks. Braising this lean protein can yield a dry, tough result, so we like to sear loin medallions and then serve them with a pan sauce made with juniper, black pepper, brandy, and cream—*steak au poivre*, new German-style. Good sides for this stick-to-your-ribs dish include Roasted Salsify with Crispy Bacon (page 150) and Potato and Sauerkraut Gratin (page 157).

INGREDIENTS (SERVES 4)

1 tsp black peppercorns

1 tsp juniper berries

1 tsp kosher salt

8 venison medallions, each about 4 oz/115 g and 1 in/ 2.5 cm thick

1 tbsp canola oil

¼ cup/60 ml brandy

¾ cup/180 ml heavy cream

1 tbsp finely chopped fresh curly-leaf parsley

1. In a spice grinder, combine the peppercorns and juniper berries and pulse until coarsely ground. Pour into a small bowl and stir in the salt. Coat the venison medallions lightly and evenly with this mixture and place on a plate.

2. In a large sauté pan, heat the canola oil over high heat. Working in batches to avoid crowding, add the medallions and cook, turning once, until nicely browned on both sides, about 3 minutes on each side. Transfer the medallions to a plate and keep warm.

3. Remove the pan from the heat, add the brandy, and allow the alcohol to cook off away from the heat to avoid flare-ups, about 1 minute. Add the cream, return the pan to medium-high heat, and cook for a few minutes until reduced by half. Stir in the parsley.

4. Return the medallions to the pan and cook, turning once, for about 1 minute. The medallions should be medium-rare. Arrange them on a platter and top with the sauce. Serve immediately.

RABBIT BRAISED IN SPICED RED WINE
WITH BLOOD SAUSAGE SAUCE
HASENPFEFFER

MANY AMERICANS know *Hasenpfeffer* from its mention in the opening credits of *Laverne & Shirley*. But we were surprised how diners clamor for this braised rabbit classic every time it is on the menu at Brauhaus Schmitz. We are going to make those people's dreams come true with this recipe for making it at home. German cooks often use hare's blood to thicken the sauce, but it is easier to find and use blood sausage, and the result is just as good. Serve this hearty braise spooned over *Schupfnudeln* (see page 174) or spaetzle (see page 168), both of which will soak up the flavors.

INGREDIENTS (SERVES 6 TO 8)

2 whole rabbits, about 3 lb/1.4 kg each

3 cups/720 ml fruity red wine

1 cup/240 ml red wine vinegar

4 fresh bay leaves, or 2 dried bay leaves

3 star anise pods

1 cinnamon stick

1 tsp coriander seeds

1 tsp black peppercorns

1 tsp whole cloves

One 3-in/7.5-cm knob fresh ginger

1 tsp juniper berries

¼ tsp whole allspice

1 cup/140 g all-purpose flour

Kosher salt and freshly ground black pepper

1 cup/220 g unsalted butter

1 lb/455 g German blood sausages, casings removed

1. Cut up each rabbit (or ask your butcher to do it for you) to yield 6 pieces: 2 forelegs, 2 hind legs, and the saddle split lengthwise. In a container large enough to accommodate both rabbits, combine the wine, vinegar, bay leaves, star anise pods, cinnamon stick, coriander seeds, peppercorns, cloves, ginger, juniper berries, and allspice and mix well. Coat the rabbit pieces thoroughly with this mixture, cover, and refrigerate for 24 hours.

2. The next day, preheat the oven to 350°F/180°C. Remove the rabbit pieces from the marinade, reserving the marinade. Pat the rabbit pieces dry with paper towels.

3. Spread the flour on a plate, season it with salt and pepper, and stir to combine. One at a time, dredge the rabbit pieces in the flour, coating them evenly, shaking off the excess, and setting them aside on another plate. Reserve the flour.

4. In a Dutch oven or other large, heavy pot with a lid, melt ½ cup/110 g of the butter over medium-high heat. Working in small batches to avoid crowding, place the rabbit pieces in the pot and cook, turning once, until browned on both sides, about 5 minutes on each side. Transfer to a plate.

5. When all of the rabbit has been browned, turn the heat to medium, and then add the remaining butter to the pot. When the butter has melted, add the reserved flour, and stir together until the flour is fully incorporated with the butter. Add the reserved marinade and the rabbit pieces and bring the liquid to a simmer. Cover the pot, transfer it to the oven, and cook until the meat is tender and easily pulls away from the bone, about 1½ hours.

6. Remove the pot from the oven. Lift the rabbit pieces from the pot, arrange on a platter, and cover to keep warm. Strain the cooking liquid through a fine-mesh sieve into a medium saucepan and discard the solids. Place the saucepan over medium-high heat and bring to a boil. Add the blood sausage, which will melt into the sauce and thicken it. Taste and adjust the seasoning with salt and pepper.

7. Pour the sauce over the rabbit and serve immediately.

6

VEGETABLES

GEMÜSE

WITH HOME GARDENING and commercial farming playing vital roles in everyday German life, it makes sense that simple vegetable preparations, ones that put natural flavor and texture first, are prevalent. You will not find many gone-modern overhauls here. Instead, you'll discover subtle updates of traditional ideas, like working green onions and parsnips into a classic potato pancake or dressing up creamed spinach or potato gratin with a few quick additions.

While the salad recipes in chapter 2 are more stand-alone or spring and summer driven, the approach here skews more toward complementing dishes with a fall and winter feel. A little heartier and a little heavier, many of these recipes are ideal for Thanksgiving, Christmas, or Sunday dinners, ideal to accompany Roasted Goose with Pretzel-Apple Stuffing and Gewürztraminer Glaze (page 105), Roasted Rack of Pork with Apple Cider Sauce (page 134), or Brisket Braised in Beer (page 120). Germans are obsessed with side dishes, so this chapter is our bid to keep them happy!

WHITE ASPARAGUS
WITH PORCINI MUSHROOM BUTTER AND ALMONDS
SPARGEL

WHITE ASPARAGUS has such a beautifully mild and sweet profile that it's not necessary to overcomplicate its preparation. Here, the spears are cooked simply and then topped with an earthy porcini-infused butter and toasted almonds.

INGREDIENTS (SERVES 4 TO 6)

1 oz/30 g dried porcini mushrooms

1 cup/225 g unsalted butter, at room temperature

Kosher salt

½ tsp freshly ground black pepper

1 tbsp finely chopped fresh curly-leaf parsley

1 lb/455 g white asparagus

¼ cup/30 g slivered blanched almonds, toasted

1. Soak the mushrooms in hot water to cover until soft, about 1 hour. Drain well, squeeze out the excess liquid, and then coarsely chop. In a food processor, combine the mushrooms, butter, 1 tsp salt, and the pepper and purée until smooth. Add the parsley and pulse just until incorporated.

2. Lay a sheet of waxed paper on a work surface. Scoop the butter mixture onto the paper, spreading it in a lengthwise strip on the sheet and leaving about 1 in/2.5 cm uncovered on each end. Roll the paper around the butter, pressing against the paper lightly to shape the butter into a long, even cylinder. Grasp the ends and twist in opposite directions to seal closed. Refrigerate the butter for up to 2 weeks. (You will need only ½ cup/115 g of the butter for this recipe. Use the remainder on grilled steaks or chops.)

3. Using a vegetable peeler, peel each asparagus spear from just below the tip to the base, removing the tough skin. Snap off the woody base from each spear where it breaks easily and then even the ends with a paring knife.

4. Fill a medium saucepan two-thirds full with water, bring to a boil over high heat, and season with salt. It should not be too salty; instead, it should be seasoned just enough to resemble a good chicken stock. Plunge the asparagus into the boiling water and cook until tender, 8 to 10 minutes; the timing depends on the size of the asparagus.

5. Drain the asparagus and arrange on a platter. Top with about ½ cup/115 g of the porcini butter and the almonds. Serve immediately.

ROASTED CAULIFLOWER
WITH EGG-AND-CRUMB CRUST
BLUMENKOHL

CAULIFLOWER, either fried or boiled and served with butter on top, is a commonplace German snack or side. This recipe is an excellent choice if you are hosting a dinner at home. Instead of individual florets, you cut a whole head of cauliflower into long slices, which you then roast with a crunchy bread-crumb crust.

INGREDIENTS (SERVES 4 TO 6)

1½ cups/120 g panko bread crumbs

3 hard-boiled eggs, peeled and chopped

2 tbsp unsalted butter, melted

2½ tsp kosher salt

1 tbsp finely chopped fresh curly-leaf parsley

1 tbsp finely chopped fresh chives

2 heads cauliflower, cored and cut lengthwise into slices ½ in/12 mm thick

2 tbsp grapeseed or canola oil

1 tsp curry powder

Leaves from 2 sprigs fresh marjoram

1. Preheat the oven to 375°F/190°C.

2. In a small bowl, combine the bread crumbs, eggs, butter, 1 tsp of the salt, the parsley, and chives and stir to mix well. Set aside.

3. In a large bowl, combine the cauliflower, grapeseed oil, curry powder, marjoram, and remaining 1½ tsp salt and toss to coat the cauliflower slices evenly with the oil and seasonings. Transfer the mixture to a 9-by-12-in/23-by-30.5-cm baking dish. Pour water to a depth of ½ in/12 mm into the dish. Cover the dish with aluminum foil.

4. Transfer the dish to the oven and bake until the cauliflower is beginning to test tender when pierced with a knife tip but is not fully cooked, about 30 minutes. Remove the dish from the oven, remove the foil, and top the cauliflower evenly with the bread crumb mixture. Return the dish, uncovered, to the oven and roast until the cauliflower is tender when pierced and the top is nicely browned, about 20 minutes longer.

5. Remove from the oven and let cool for a few minutes before serving.

BARLEY-AND-MUSHROOM-STUFFED KOHLRABI

GEFÜLLTES KOHLRABI

ALTHOUGH THIS CHAPTER IS BIG ON SIDE DISHES, this recipe is flavorful enough to stand alone as a main course. Kohlrabi, that wonderful baseball-size German turnip, has had a special place in the German culinary repertoire for centuries. Stuffed kohlrabi is usually filled with sausage, but here, barley, toasted ahead of time to draw out its appealing nuttiness, has taken its place. The sauce is made with Riesling that is added to the baking pan with the kohlrabies.

INGREDIENTS (SERVES 8)

1 cup/200 g pearl barley

4 cups/960 ml water

8 kohlrabies, each about 3 in/7.5 cm in diameter

Kosher salt

1 tbsp canola oil

1 tbsp unsalted butter

1 yellow onion, diced

4 garlic cloves, minced

2 portobello mushrooms, trimmed and sliced

1 tbsp finely chopped fresh rosemary

1 tbsp finely chopped fresh marjoram, or 1 tsp dried marjoram

1 tbsp finely chopped fresh curly-leaf parsley

1 tsp sweet Hungarian paprika

¼ cup/60 ml fresh lemon juice

½ tsp freshly ground black pepper

1½ cups/360 ml Riesling

½ cup/120 ml crème fraîche

1 tbsp cornstarch

1. Preheat the oven to 375°F/190°C.

2. Spread the barley on a rimmed sheet pan and toast in the oven until golden brown, about 15 minutes. Transfer the barley to a medium saucepan, add the water, cover, and bring to a boil over high heat. Lower the heat to a simmer and cook until the barley is tender, about 30 minutes. Remove from the heat, drain, and transfer the cooked barley to a sheet pan. Let cool completely.

3. Using a vegetable peeler, remove the tough outer layer of each kohlrabi bulb. Identify the top end and bottom end of each bulb—the bottom is much woodier—and cut off a thin slice from each end with a sharp knife. Make sure the bottom is even so the kohlrabi will stand upright.

4. Using a melon baller or a small spoon, and working from the top of the bulb, scoop out the insides of each kohlrabi, leaving a shell ½ in/ 12 mm thick. Set aside 1 cup/300 g of the removed kohlrabi flesh for the stuffing and reserve the remainder for another use.

(Continued)

5. Fill a medium stockpot two-thirds full with water, season with enough salt to resemble seawater, and bring to a boil over high heat. Add the kohlrabi shells, turn the heat to medium, and simmer until a knife inserted into a shell meets some resistance, about 15 minutes. The shells should be soft enough to finish cooking in the oven but not so soft that they will collapse. Meanwhile, line a large plate with paper towels. When the kohlrabi shells are ready, using a slotted spoon, transfer them to the towel-lined plate, inverting them to drain.

6. Once again, preheat the oven to 375°F/190°C.

7. Chop the reserved kohlrabi flesh. In a medium sauté pan, heat the canola oil and butter over medium-high heat. Add the onion and garlic and cook, stirring occasionally, until translucent, about 4 minutes. Add the mushrooms and chopped kohlrabi and continue to cook, stirring often, until the mushrooms are softened and the kohlrabi is tender, about 6 minutes. Add the rosemary, marjoram, and parsley and stir to combine. Remove the pan from the heat and pour the contents into a medium bowl. Add the cooked barley, paprika, lemon juice, 2 tsp salt, and the pepper to the bowl and mix together until thoroughly combined.

8. Stuff the kohlrabi shells with the barley mixture, dividing it evenly. Arrange the kohlrabies in a baking dish just large enough to accommodate them. Pour the Riesling into the bottom of the dish and place in the oven.

9. Bake the kohlrabies until they are tender when pierced with a knife, about 30 minutes. Using a slotted spoon, remove the stuffed kohlrabies to a platter and cover to keep warm, reserving the liquid.

10. Pour the reserved liquid in the baking dish into a small saucepan, place over medium-high heat, and bring to a gentle boil. In a small bowl, stir together the crème fraîche and cornstarch. Whisk the mixture into the liquid in the saucepan and cook, stirring constantly, until slightly thickened, about 3 minutes.

11. Pour the sauce over the kohlrabies and serve immediately.

ROASTED SALSIFY WITH CRISPY BACON

SCHWARZWURZELN

SCHWARZWURZELN—"black roots"—are popular in Germany and are also widely eaten in Belgium, the Netherlands, and other European countries. But they are less commonly cooked in the United States, where they are known as salsify. This hearty root vegetable has the texture of a firm potato and an unmistakable flavor that is best described as reminiscent of a briny artichoke, and is ideal for roasting. When you peel salsify, be sure to wear gloves, as it releases a sticky substance that is difficult to get off your hands.

INGREDIENTS (SERVES 4 TO 6)

8 salsify roots, peeled

1 tsp kosher salt

Juice of 1 lemon

2 fresh bay leaves, or 1 dried bay leaf

1 tbsp grapeseed or canola oil

6 slices thick-cut bacon, diced

1 yellow onion, sliced

2 garlic cloves, minced

Leaves from 4 sprigs fresh thyme

½ tsp freshly ground black pepper

1. In a medium saucepan, combine the salsify, salt, lemon juice, bay leaves, and water to cover and bring to a boil over high heat. Turn the heat to a simmer and cook, uncovered, until the salsify is almost tender when pierced with a knife, about 6 minutes. Meanwhile, line a plate with paper towels.

2. When the salsify is ready, remove from the heat. Using a slotted spoon, transfer the roots to the towel-lined plate to drain. When cool enough to handle, cut the roots in half lengthwise, then cut crosswise into pieces about 5 in/12 cm long. Arrange the pieces in a single layer on a small sheet pan or in a small baking dish.

3. Preheat the oven to 350°F/180°C.

4. In a medium frying pan, heat the grapeseed oil and bacon over medium-high heat and cook until the bacon renders some of its fat and starts to brown, about 4 minutes. Add the onion and garlic and cook, stirring, for 2 minutes longer. Stir in the thyme and pepper, remove the pan from the heat, and pour the mixture evenly over the salsify.

5. Bake the salsify until lightly browned, about 15 minutes. Remove from the oven and serve immediately.

RADISHES
BRAISED IN CHICKEN STOCK, BUTTER, AND THYME
RADIESCHEN

RADISHES ARE EVERYWHERE IN GERMANY, though it's rare to find them cooked. *Radi,* for example, is a traditional beer-garden snack of spiral-cut white radish shavings dressed with only salt. Radishes also turn up raw in salads (see page 59). But when you braise radishes, as we do here, they take on a completely different flavor—milder, almost turnipy in this case. This is the perfect dish for people who typically don't eat radishes because of their natural spiciness. Serve it alongside Pilsner-and-Pickle-Juice-Brined Roasted Chicken (page 102).

INGREDIENTS (SERVES 4 TO 6)

2 bunches red radishes

1 tbsp grapeseed or canola oil

2 shallots, sliced

2 garlic cloves, sliced

1 cup/240 ml chicken stock, low sodium if store-bought

Leaves from 6 sprigs fresh thyme

1 tsp kosher salt

3 tbsp unsalted butter

1 tbsp finely chopped fresh curly-leaf parsley

1. Remove the green tops from the radish bunches, coarsely chop the tops, and set them aside. Cut the radishes in half lengthwise.

2. In a medium saucepan, heat the grapeseed oil over medium-high heat. Add the shallots and garlic and cook, stirring frequently, until lightly browned, about 4 minutes. Add the halved radishes, stir to combine, and cook for 2 minutes. Pour in the stock, bring to a boil, and turn the heat to a simmer. Add the thyme and salt and simmer for 5 minutes. Add the reserved radish tops and continue to simmer until the radishes and the tops are tender, about 5 minutes longer. At this point, the stock should be reduced by half.

3. Using a slotted spoon, transfer the radishes and the tops to a bowl. Remove the pan from the heat and whisk the butter into the reduced stock. Return the radishes and the tops to the pan and mix them with the sauce.

4. Transfer the mixture to a serving dish and garnish with the parsley. Serve immediately.

CREAMED SPINACH
WITH MUSHROOMS AND CRISPY SHALLOTS
RAHMSPINAT

IF YOU LOVE traditional American steakhouse creamed spinach as a side, you'll love this dish. Making your own fried shallots is ideal, but if you're short on time, you can swap in store-bought fried onions with similar results.

INGREDIENTS (SERVES 4)

CRISPY SHALLOTS

2 tbsp all-purpose flour

1 tbsp cornstarch

1 tsp kosher salt

4 shallots, thinly sliced lengthwise

¼ cup/60 ml canola oil

1 tbsp canola oil

1 tbsp unsalted butter

2 shallots, sliced

2 garlic cloves, minced

8 oz/225 g portobello mush-rooms, trimmed and sliced

1 lb/455 g baby spinach

¼ tsp freshly grated nutmeg

1 tsp kosher salt

½ cup/120 ml heavy cream

1. *To make the shallots,* in a medium bowl, stir together the flour, cornstarch, and salt, mixing well. Dredge the shallots in the flour mixture, shaking off any excess. In a medium sauté pan, heat the canola oil over medium-high heat. When the oil is hot, gently drop in the shallots and fry, stirring occasionally, until golden brown and crispy, about 4 minutes. Using a slotted spoon, transfer to paper towels to drain.

2. In a large sauté pan, heat the 1 tbsp canola oil and butter over medium-high heat. Add the 2 shallots and the garlic and cook, stirring occasionally, until translucent, about 4 minutes. Add the mushrooms and cook, stirring occasionally, for 4 minutes. Add the spinach, nutmeg, salt, and cream and stir and toss to mix. Turn the heat to low and simmer gently until the cream has reduced by half, about 8 minutes.

3. Transfer the spinach to a serving dish and top with the shallots. Serve immediately.

SAVOY CABBAGE
BRAISED IN CIDER
WITH GREEN APPLES AND LEEKS
WIRSING

SOME FOLKS are surprised to discover that cabbage is more than just sauerkraut in Germany. This dish is a good side for autumn, as it features hard cider and apples, two cool-weather favorites. The flavors remind us of Frankfurt, where *Apfelwein* (apple wine) flows as freely as beer.

INGREDIENTS (SERVES 4)

1 tbsp canola oil

1 tbsp unsalted butter

2 leeks, white and green parts, cut into slices 1 in/2.5 cm thick

4 green apples, halved, cored, and cut into slices ½ in/12 mm thick

1 head Savoy cabbage, cored and finely shredded

2 cups/480 ml hard cider

1 tbsp cider vinegar

2 tsp kosher salt

1 tbsp sugar

¼ tsp freshly ground black pepper

Leaves from 4 sprigs fresh thyme

¼ cup/25 g chopped walnuts

1. In a large frying pan, heat the canola oil and butter over medium-high heat. Add the leeks and cook, stirring often, until softened, about 4 minutes. Add the apples and continue to cook for 2 minutes. Using a slotted spoon, transfer the leeks and apples to a medium bowl and reserve.

2. Add the cabbage, cider, vinegar, salt, sugar, pepper, and thyme to the same pan over medium-high heat, bring to a boil, turn the heat to a simmer, and cook until the cabbage is tender, about 15 minutes. Return the leeks and apples to the pan, stir to combine, and cook until the apples and leeks are heated through, about 3 minutes. The apples should remain crunchy.

3. Transfer to a platter and top with the walnuts. Serve immediately.

ROASTED BRUSSELS SPROUTS
WITH SMOKED SAUSAGE AND SHALLOTS
ROSENKOHL

THIS DISH has been on the Brauhaus Schmitz winter menu since we opened in 2009. Plenty of people are convinced that they don't like Brussels sprouts, but it's hard to say no to these little cabbages when they are roasted until they are deliciously caramelized—an ideal mix of soft and crispy. When Jeremy was growing up, the only way he ever ate Brussels sprouts was thoroughly doused in a nice balsamic vinegar, a move his grandfather taught him. That's why a little acid has been introduced here, in the form of sherry or balsamic vinegar. When buying the sausage for this side, remember that the smokier it is, the better.

INGREDIENTS (SERVES 4 TO 6)

1 tbsp kosher salt, plus 1 tsp

1 lb/455 g Brussels sprouts, cut in half lengthwise

1 tbsp canola oil

1 smoked sausage such as Bauernwurst or kielbasa, sliced

2 shallots or 1 small yellow onion, sliced

½ tsp freshly cracked black pepper

1 tbsp unsalted butter

1 tbsp sherry vinegar or balsamic vinegar

1. Preheat the oven to 375°F/190°C.

2. Fill a medium pot three-fourths full with water, bring to a boil over high heat, and add the 1 tbsp salt. Plunge the sprouts into the boiling water and cook until they start to feel tender when pierced with a knife tip, 8 to 10 minutes; the timing will depend on their size. Drain the sprouts well.

3. In a medium cast-iron or other heavy frying pan, heat the canola oil over medium-high heat. Working in batches if necessary to avoid crowding, add the sprouts, cut-side down and in a single layer, and cook until they are browned on the bottom, about 6 minutes. Transfer to a plate and reserve.

4. Add the sausage, shallots, remaining 1 tsp salt, pepper, and butter to the same pan, turn the heat to medium, and cook, stirring occasionally, until the shallots are softened, about 5 minutes.

5. Return the sprouts to the pan, add the vinegar, and toss together all of the ingredients. Transfer the pan to the oven and roast until the sprouts are tender when pierced with the tip of a knife and browned, about 10 minutes.

6. Transfer to a serving dish and serve immediately.

POTATO, PARSNIP, AND GREEN ONION PANCAKES

KARTOFFELPUFFER

POTATO PANCAKES are eaten everywhere in Germany, and they appear under many different names, depending on the region in which they are made. They are popular at Brauhaus Schmitz, too, where many diners are surprised that ours, unlike most latkes, are gluten-free: we use potato starch in place of wheat flour (cornstarch will work, too). The nontraditional addition of parsnips introduces an appealing sweet note that contrasts well with the seasonings here.

INGREDIENTS (SERVES 4 TO 6)

2 Yukon gold potatoes

3 parsnips

1 bunch green onions, white and green parts, sliced

3 eggs, lightly beaten

1½ tsp kosher salt

½ tsp ground white pepper

¼ tsp freshly grated nutmeg

2 tbsp potato starch or cornstarch, or more if needed

½ cup/120 ml canola oil

½ cup/115 g unsalted butter

Sour cream, whisked to loosen, for serving

Applesauce for serving

1. Peel the potatoes and shred them on the large holes of a box grater into a bowl of cold water. Peel and shred the parsnips the same way. Drain the potatoes and parsnips, rinse them with cold water, and then squeeze them with your hands to remove as much moisture as possible.

2. In a large bowl, combine the potatoes, parsnips, green onions, eggs, salt, white pepper, and nutmeg and mix well. Add the potato starch and stir to mix. The mixture should hold together while still being slightly loose. If the mixture is too crumbly, add more potato starch, small pinches at a time, until the mixture holds together.

3. In a large cast-iron or other heavy frying pan, heat the canola oil and butter over medium-high heat. While the fat is heating, form the potato mixture into cakes about 4 in/10 cm in diameter and ¼ in/6 mm thick. Carefully place the cakes in the hot fat, fitting as many as you can in the pan without crowding them. Using the back of a spoon or spatula, flatten the tops, then cook, turning once, until cooked through and nicely browned on both sides, 3 to 4 minutes on each side. Using a slotted spatula, transfer them to a heatproof platter and keep them warm in a low oven. Cook the remaining cakes in the same way.

4. Serve the cakes hot, drizzled with sour cream and accompanied with applesauce.

POTATO AND SAUERKRAUT GRATIN

KARTOFFEL-SAUERKRAUT GRATIN

A POTATO GRATIN is often on the menu of a Sunday supper in Germany, usually alongside a big roast or stew. At Brauhaus Schmitz, sauerkraut makes a surprise appearance in our potato gratin. The starch from the raw potatoes nicely thickens the garlic-laced cream mixture, the richness of which is cut by the natural sourness of the kraut. You certainly don't need to top this gratin with cheese, but if you decide to do it, use Parmesan or aged Gouda—you probably won't hear any complaints.

INGREDIENTS (SERVES 4 TO 6)

2 tbsp unsalted butter, at room temperature

2½ cups/600 ml heavy cream

3 garlic cloves, sliced

1½ tbsp kosher salt

½ tsp freshly grated nutmeg

5 russet potatoes, peeled and sliced as thinly as possible

About 1 lb/455 g sauerkraut, homemade (see page 194) or store-bought, drained

1. Preheat the oven to 300°F/150°C. Grease a 9-by-12-in/23-by-30.5-cm baking dish with the butter.

2. In a medium saucepan, combine the cream, garlic, salt, and nutmeg over medium heat and heat until the mixture is hot but not boiling. Keep your eye on the pan as the mixture heats, as it can quickly go from hot to boiling over, and remove it from the heat the moment the mixture is hot.

3. Arrange half of the potato slices in a layer in the prepared baking dish. Spoon the sauerkraut in an even layer over the potatoes, then layer the remaining potato slices on top. Pour the cream mixture evenly over the layers.

4. Bake the gratin until the potatoes are tender when pierced with a knife tip, about 45 minutes. Remove from the oven and let cool for about 15 minutes before serving.

NOODLES & DUMPLINGS

NUDELN UND KNÖDEL

SPAETZLE is the most beloved and recognizable of Germany's noodle dishes—we go through 100 to 200 lb/45 to 90 kg a week at the restaurant—but there is more to German pasta than the hundreds of variations on "little sparrows." Eastern European–style dumplings, from plain dough cooked in soup broth to versions filled with potato and other vegetables or meats, are common, as are wide, flat egg noodles similar to Italian *tagliatelle* or *pappardelle*. Dig deeper into regional specialties and you'll find filled pastas like *Maultaschen* and even a German version of pierogi called *Schlutzkrapfen*. Yes, spaetzle is king, but there are other members of the Teutonic carb court worthy of your fork's attention.

RYE EGG NOODLES

ROGGENNUDELN

ROLLED OUT BY HAND to ¼ in/6 mm thick, then cut by hand into irregular diamonds, *Roggennudeln* fall somewhere between dumplings and noodles in their shape and their texture. They are most frequently used in soup broths, but this nutty-flavored tweener pasta goes well with a braise, a stew, or the sauce from a roast, as well. You can also toss them with butter and chives and serve them as a simple side dish to chops or steaks.

INGREDIENTS (MAKES ABOUT 1 LB/455 G NOODLES)

1½ cups/150 g medium rye flour

1 cup/140 g all-purpose flour, plus more for dusting

3 eggs, lightly beaten

½ cup/120 ml water

1 tbsp grapeseed or canola oil, plus more as needed if reserving the noodles

Kosher salt

1. In a stand mixer fitted with the paddle attachment, mix together the rye flour and all-purpose flour on low speed. Add the eggs, water, and grapeseed oil and continue to mix on low speed for 1 minute. Increase the speed to medium and mix until the dough comes together, 2 to 3 minutes. Increase the mixer speed by one setting and continue mixing until all of the ingredients are thoroughly combined and a tight dough ball has formed, about 5 minutes.

2. Remove the dough from the bowl, wrap in plastic wrap, and let sit at room temperature for 1 hour. (The dough can also be wrapped and refrigerated overnight; bring to room temperature before continuing.)

3. Lightly flour a work surface. Unwrap the dough and cut it into four equal portions. Place one portion on the floured work surface and roll out to ¼ in/6 mm thick. (Alternatively, following the manufacturer's instructions, roll out the dough on a pasta machine.) Using a pizza cutter or a knife, cut the dough sheet into diamond shapes about 1 in/2.5 cm long. Transfer the diamonds to a sheet pan and dust lightly with all-purpose flour. Repeat with the remaining dough portions.

4. Fill a large pot three-fourths full with water, season the water with enough salt to make it almost as salty as seawater, and bring to a boil over high heat. Drop in the noodles, stir to prevent them from sticking together, and cook until tender, 4 to 5 minutes. Drain the noodles and serve as desired, or toss with a little oil and reserve until needed.

SEMOLINA EGG NOODLES
GRIESSBANDNUDELN

YOUR STANDARD-ISSUE wide egg noodle, *Griessbandnudeln* is eaten throughout Germany. Here, the typical semolina dough is cut into broad diamonds rather than ribbons. Serve the noodles simply tossed with butter and herbs, or toss them with a gravy or the sauce from a braise.

INGREDIENTS (MAKES ABOUT 1¼ LB/565 G NOODLES)

3 cups/500 g semolina flour, plus more for dusting

3 eggs, lightly beaten

½ cup/120 ml water

1 tbsp grapeseed or canola oil, plus more as needed if reserving the noodles

Kosher salt

1. In a stand mixer fitted with the paddle attachment, combine the flour, eggs, water, and grapeseed oil and mix on low speed for 1 minute. Increase the speed to medium and mix until the dough comes together, 2 to 3 minutes. Increase the mixer speed by one setting and continue mixing until all of the ingredients are thoroughly combined and a tight dough ball forms, about 5 minutes. (If the dough feels too dry, add an additional 1 tbsp water.)

2. Remove the dough from the bowl, wrap in plastic wrap, and let sit at room temperature for 1 hour. (The dough can also be wrapped and refrigerated overnight; bring to room temperature before continuing.)

3. Lightly flour a work surface. Unwrap the dough and cut it into four equal portions. Place one portion on the floured work surface and roll out to ¼ in/6 mm thick. (Alternatively, following the manufacturer's instructions, roll out the dough on a pasta machine.) Using a pizza cutter or a knife, cut the dough sheet into diamond shapes about 1 in/2.5 cm long. Transfer the diamonds to a sheet pan and dust lightly with all-purpose flour. Repeat with the remaining dough portions.

4. Fill a large pot three-fourths full with water, season the water with enough salt to make it almost as salty as seawater, and bring to a boil over high heat. Drop in the noodles, stir to prevent them from sticking together, and cook until tender, 4 to 5 minutes. Drain the noodles and serve as desired, or toss with a little oil and reserve until needed.

SEMOLINA NOODLES WITH SAVOY CABBAGE AND ONIONS

KRAUTFLECKERL

THIS WINTRY, SATISFYING DISH can be made with store-bought fresh egg noodles or, if you have time, you can make your own. Regardless of which direction you go, remember to pull the noodles out of the pasta water slightly before they are done and transfer them into the pot with the onions and cabbage. This will ensure they absorb as much flavor as possible as they finish cooking. *Krautfleckerl* makes for an excellent side for sausages like Spicy Hungarian-Style Bratwurst (page 114) or Smoked Pork and Bacon Sausage (page 110), though it's hearty enough to stand alone also as a vegetarian main course.

INGREDIENTS (SERVES 4)

1 tbsp canola oil

½ cup/110 g unsalted butter

1 yellow onion, diced

½ head Savoy cabbage, cored and cut into 1-in/2.5-cm squares

1½ tbsp sugar

1 tbsp finely chopped fresh marjoram, or 1 tsp dried marjoram

Kosher salt

12 oz/340 g fresh semolina egg noodles, homemade (see page 163) or store-bought

Freshly ground black pepper

1. In a medium Dutch oven, heat the canola oil and butter over medium-high heat. Add the onion and cook, stirring occasionally, until lightly browned, about 10 minutes. Add the cabbage, sugar, marjoram, and 1½ tsp salt and stir to combine. Turn the heat to low and cook until the cabbage is soft, about 20 minutes.

2. Meanwhile, fill a large pot three-fourths full with water, season the water with enough salt to make it almost as salty as seawater, and bring to a boil over high heat. Drop in the noodles, stir to prevent them from sticking together, and cook until almost tender, 3 to 4 minutes. (They will cook more with the cabbage mixture.)

3. Drain the noodles, add them to the cabbage mixture, and continue to cook, stirring occasionally, until heated through and the noodles have absorbed some flavor from the cabbage mixture, about 6 minutes. Season with salt and pepper and serve immediately.

BUCKWHEAT SPAETZLE

BUCHWEIZEN SPÄTZLE

A MIX OF BUCKWHEAT and bread flours for spaetzle dough gives the dumplings a slightly unexpected flavor profile. There are two common ways to shape the dough into spaetzle. If you want to be traditional, it's customary to use a *Spätzlebrett*, or "spaetzle board," which allows you to flick long, skinny strands of the dough into boiling water. But you can also use a spaetzle press, which forces the dough through holes in a small box or cylinder into the water and is a faster and more beginner-friendly option. If you do not already own a spaetzle press, look for one at a well-stocked cookware store or online.

If you're preparing a large amount of spaetzle to be served later, ready an ice-water bath in a large bowl and shock the noodles in the ice bath as they come out of the boiling water. For traditional spaetzle, use 3 cups/420 g all-purpose flour in place of the buckwheat and bread flour and prepare the dough as directed. When you cook the noodles, remove them from the water as soon as they rise to top. Hearty buckwheat flour requires longer cooking.

Serve the freshly boiled spaetzle tossed with butter, or brown them lightly in butter in a frying pan and garnish with chopped fresh chives. Spaetzle is also delicious served with stews or braises, with creamy sauces, or tossed with butter and cheese.

INGREDIENTS (SERVES 4)

5 eggs

½ cup/120 ml buttermilk

2 tbsp canola or grapeseed oil, plus more for oiling the bowl

2 cups/250 g buckwheat flour

1 cup/135 g bread flour or all-purpose flour

¼ tsp freshly grated nutmeg

Kosher salt

1. In a medium bowl, whisk the eggs until well blended. Whisk in the buttermilk and canola oil.

2. In the bowl of a stand mixer fitted with the dough hook, combine the buckwheat flour, bread flour, nutmeg, and ¼ tsp salt and mix on low speed for 1 minute. Slowly add the egg mixture and continue to mix on low speed until the dough resembles a somewhat thick, sticky batter, 2 to 3 minutes.

(Continued)

3. Remove the bowl from the mixer stand and let the dough rest for about 15 minutes. While you are waiting, fill a large saucepan or medium stockpot half full with water and bring to a boil over high heat. Season the water with salt, keeping in mind that the more salt you add, the saltier the spaetzle will be. When the water is at a good boil, lower the heat so the water is at a steady simmer just under a boil. (If the water is boiling too rapidly, the spaetzle will fall apart.) Oil a medium bowl and set it near the stove top.

4. Transfer as much dough as will fit comfortably in the spaetzle press, push the dough into the water, and give the water a quick stir so the pieces don't stick together. Once the spaetzle rises to the top, let simmer for 3 minutes longer, then scoop out the pieces with a slotted spoon and drop them into the oiled bowl. Repeat until all of the dough has been cooked, then serve as desired.

SPAETZLE WITH HAM, PEAS, CREAM, AND AGED GOUDA

SCHINKENSPÄTZLE

A LITTLE CREAMY, a little salty, and plenty satisfying, this dish is probably as close as you're going to come to German carbonara. Westphalian ham, naturally cured and heavily smoked, plays the role of *guanciale* here; if you can't get your hands on the ham, Italian speck makes a good substitute. Although store-bought spaetzle will work here, we recommend that you make it yourself once you are comfortable with the process.

INGREDIENTS (SERVES 4)

1 tbsp canola oil, plus more for oiling the bowl

4 oz/115 g Westphalian ham or Italian speck, thinly sliced, then cut into narrow strips

1 garlic clove, minced

2 green onions, white and green parts, sliced

1 cup/140 g fresh or frozen shelled English peas

1 recipe Buckwheat Spaetzle (page 168), or 1 lb/455 g dried spaetzle, cooked

¼ cup/60 ml heavy cream

1 tbsp finely chopped fresh curly-leaf parsley

Aged Gouda or Prima Donna cheese for grating

1. In a medium nonstick frying pan, heat the canola oil over medium-high heat. Add the ham and garlic and cook, stirring occasionally, until the ham is lightly browned, about 3 minutes. Add the green onions and peas and continue to cook until the onions are transluscent, about 5 minutes longer. Add the cooked spaetzle and cream, stir to mix evenly, and cook, stirring occasionally, just until the spaetzle is heated through, about 5 minutes.

2. Sprinkle with the parsley, stir to combine, and transfer to a platter. Grate some Gouda over the top and serve immediately.

SPAETZLE WITH ASPARAGUS, AGED GOUDA, AND RAMP-HAZELNUT PESTO

GEMÜSESPÄTZLE

THIS SPAETZLE DISH is all about spring—the asparagus, the ramps, the light and refreshing character of the dish. If you cannot find both white and green asparagus, it's fine to use only one or the other. What really jumps out in this dish is the ramp-hazelnut pesto, which is equal parts garlicky zing and nutty warmth. If you cannot locate ramps, you can substitute 3 green onions, white and green parts, and 2 garlic cloves.

INGREDIENTS (SERVES 4)

PESTO

¼ cup/35 g blanched hazelnuts

4 ramps, bulbs and leaves, roughly chopped

⅓ cup/40 g grated aged Gouda or Prima Donna cheese, plus 1½ tbsp

8 oz/225 g green asparagus (or 1 lb/450 g if using green only)

8 oz/225 g white asparagus (optional)

1 tbsp canola oil, plus more for oiling the bowl

1 tbsp unsalted butter

1 recipe Buckwheat Spaetzle (page 168), or 1 lb/455 g dried spaetzle, cooked

2 tbsp finely chopped fresh curly-leaf parsley

Kosher salt and freshly ground black pepper

1. *To make the pesto,* preheat the oven to 350°F/180°C. Spread the hazelnuts on a small sheet pan or a pie pan and toast until golden brown, about 20 minutes. Remove from the oven and let cool.

2. In a food processor, process the ramps until smooth. Add the hazelnuts and ⅓ cup/40 g Gouda and pulse until combined but the mixture is still a little coarse. Transfer to a bowl, stir in the remaining 1½ tbsp Gouda, cover, and refrigerate until ready to use.

3. Using a vegetable peeler, peel each asparagus spear from just below the tip to the base, removing the tough skin. Snap off the woody base from each spear where it breaks easily and then even

the ends with a paring knife. Cut crosswise on the diagonal into bite-size pieces. Set aside.

4. In a large sauté pan, combine the canola oil and butter over medium-high heat. Add all of the asparagus and cook, stirring occasionally, until nearly tender, 5 to 6 minutes. Add the spaetzle and stir to combine thoroughly and heat through, a few minutes longer. Stir in the parsley and season with salt and pepper.

5. Remove from the heat, add half of the pesto to the spaetzle and asparagus, and toss and stir to mix well. Transfer to a platter, spoon the remaining pesto on top, and serve immediately.

QUARK CHEESE, POTATO, AND HERB DUMPLINGS

SCHUPFNUDELN

THESE DUMPLINGS are cousins of Italian gnocchi. We start by blending a potato base with quark cheese, the plain, rennet-free curded product similar to *fromage blanc* (farmer cheese, mascarpone cheese, or Greek yogurt also works well here). The shape of German gnocchi, fat in the middle and tapered at each end, as opposed to uniformly plump little pillows, distinguishes them from their Italian relatives. Be careful not to overwork the dough or your dumplings will be chewy. Because they soak up sauce so well, these dumplings are a perfect side for Brisket Braised in Beer (page 120).

INGREDIENTS (SERVES 4 TO 6)

Kosher salt

2 lb/910 g russet potatoes

½ cup/70 g all-purpose flour, plus more for dusting

¼ tsp freshly grated nutmeg

1 tbsp finely chopped fresh curly-leaf parsley

1 tbsp finely chopped fresh chives

1 egg, lightly beaten

4 oz/115 g quark or farmer cheese

2 tbsp canola oil

1 tbsp unsalted butter

1. Fill a large pot two-thirds full with water, add enough salt for the water to taste like seawater, and bring to a boil over high heat. Slip the potatoes into the boiling water, return the water to a boil, adjust the heat to maintain a steady simmer, and cook until a knife inserted into a potato meets no resistance, 25 to 30 minutes.

2. Drain the potatoes into a colander and let cool just until they can be handled, then peel them. Pass the warm potatoes through a ricer held over a large bowl, or place the potatoes in the bowl and mash with a potato masher until smooth.

3. Add the flour, nutmeg, 1 tsp salt, the parsley, and chives and stir to combine. Fold in the egg and cheese just until evenly mixed. Knead the dough gently in the bowl until smooth, pliable, and moist but not too wet. (To test if the dough has the correct consistency, bring a small saucepan of water to a boil and drop a little nugget of the dough into the water. If the nugget falls apart, add a little more flour to the dough.)

4. Lightly flour a work surface. Transfer the dough to the floured surface and roll out to about ½ in/12 mm thick. Cut the dough into strips about 1½ in/4 cm long and ½ in/12 mm wide.

Using your index finger and pinky, gently taper both ends of each strip. Each dumpling should be thicker at the center and pointed at the ends. Dust a sheet pan with flour and transfer the dumplings to the pan. Set aside for 15 minutes.

5. Refill the large pot three-fourths full with water, season with enough salt to resemble seawater, and bring to a boil over high heat. Add the dumplings, adjust the heat to maintain a gentle boil, and cook for 8 minutes. Using a slotted spoon or skimmer, lift out the dumplings, draining them well, and transfer to a shallow dish. Let cool completely, then cover the dumplings and refrigerate overnight.

6. The next day, in a large frying pan, heat the canola oil and butter over medium heat. Place as many dumplings as will fit in a single layer in the pan and fry, turning once, until golden brown on both sides, 6 to 8 minutes total. Using a slotted spoon, carefully transfer the dumplings to a serving dish and keep warm while you cook the remaining dumplings. Serve immediately.

PRETZEL DUMPLING WITH SMOKED SAUSAGE

BREZELKNÖDEL

ALTHOUGH OUR PRETZELS ARE SO GOOD that we seldom have any left over, when we do, *Brezelknödel* is easily our favorite thing to make with them. We soak day-old pretzels in hot milk, mash them, and then mix the mash with diced smoky sausage (we use *Landjäger* sausage, which is common to southern Germany) and form the mixture into balls. You can either poach the dumplings and eat them as is, or you can take the extra step of crisping them in a hot pan. You can also shape the mixture into a log, poach the log, allow it to cool, and then slice it and crisp the slices in a hot pan. This is an excellent cold-weather side that pairs well with Venison Medallions with Juniper–Black Pepper Brandy Sauce (page 139) or Chicken Braised in Riesling (page 101).

INGREDIENTS

1 cup/240 ml whole milk

3 cups/185 g cut-up day-old soft pretzels (1-in/2.5-cm pieces), homemade (see page 18) or store-bought

1 tbsp canola oil

1 tbsp unsalted butter, plus more as needed if panfrying dumplings

1 yellow onion, diced

2 garlic cloves, minced

4 Landjäger or other smoked sausages (about 5 oz/140 g total weight), cut into small pieces

1 tbsp finely chopped fresh marjoram

1 tbsp finely chopped fresh curly-leaf parsley

3 eggs, lightly beaten

¼ cup/35 g all-purpose flour

1½ tsp kosher salt

½ tsp freshly ground black pepper

1. In a small saucepan, heat the milk over medium heat until it almost comes to a simmer. Meanwhile, put the pretzels in a medium bowl. When the milk is ready, pour it over the pretzels and set aside.

2. In a medium sauté pan, heat the canola oil and butter over medium-high heat. Add the onion and garlic and cook, stirring occasionally, until lightly browned, about 6 minutes. Add the sausages, marjoram, and parsley and cook, stirring, for another 5 minutes to blend the flavors. Remove the pan from the heat and let the sausage mixture cool completely.

3. In a large bowl, combine the milk-soaked pretzels and the sausage mixture and mix thoroughly. Add the eggs, flour, salt, and pepper and stir until all of the ingredients are evenly incorporated.

4. There are two ways to make the dumplings: you can shape the mixture into small balls and poach the balls in simmering water, or you can roll the entire mixture into a log shape, called a *Serviettenknödel* (napkin dumpling), wrap the log in plastic wrap, and poach it. Fill a large pot two-thirds full with water and bring to a boil over high heat.

To make the ball-type dumplings, roll the mixture into balls slightly larger than a golf ball, place them on a sheet pan, cover, and refrigerate for 1 hour. Then, gently drop the balls into the boiling water, turn the heat to a gentle simmer, and cook for 25 minutes. Do not let the water boil or the dumplings will fall apart. To test for doneness, scoop out a dumpling from the pot and insert a cake tester or thin skewer into the center. If it comes out with no egg residue clinging to it, the dumplings are ready. Using a slotted spoon, transfer the dumplings to a platter and serve immediately. Or, if you like, you can crisp the poached dumplings in butter in a hot pan.

To make the napkin-type dumpling, lay a sheet of plastic wrap on a work surface. Turn the mixture out onto the plastic wrap and shape it into a log about 8 in/20 cm long and 2 in/5 cm in diameter. Roll up the log tightly in the plastic wrap and tie each end with kitchen string. Lower the log into the boiling water, turn the heat to a gentle simmer, and cook for 25 minutes. To test for doneness, retrieve the log from the water and test with a cake tester or thin skewer. If it comes out with no egg residue clinging to it, the dumpling is ready. Let cool completely and refrigerate overnight. The next day, unwrap the log, cut it into slices, and panfry the slices in butter until heated through to serve.

POTATO, SPINACH, AND SAUERKRAUT PIEROGI
WITH BROWN BUTTER AND SOUR CREAM
SCHLUTZKRAPFEN

ALTHOUGH THEY ARE NOT CALLED *PIEROGI* in Germany, *Schlutzkrapfen* are nearly the twin of one of Poland's most recognizable food exports. Eaten widely in southern Germany and in Austria, these dumplings differ in makeup from their European counterparts like Italian ravioli, with a generally softer dough. This recipe, built around piquant smoked sauerkraut, makes an excellent side for Nuremberg-Style Bratwurst (page 116).

INGREDIENTS (SERVES 4 TO 6)

FILLING

Kosher salt

1 lb/455 g Yukon gold potatoes

1 tbsp unsalted butter

1 yellow onion, finely chopped

2 garlic cloves, minced

6 oz/170 g spinach, chopped

6 oz/170 g sauerkraut, homemade (see page 194) or store-bought, drained

2 tbsp grated Parmesan cheese

DOUGH

1¼ cups/175 g all-purpose flour, plus more for dusting

1 cup plus 2 tbsp/115 g medium rye flour

2 eggs, lightly beaten

½ cup/120 ml water

1 tbsp canola or grapeseed oil

Kosher salt

Canola or grapeseed oil for oiling and browning the dumplings

½ cup/115 g unsalted butter

½ cup/120 ml sour cream

1. *To make the filling,* fill a medium pot two-thirds full with water, add enough salt for the water to taste like seawater, and bring to a boil over high heat. Slip the potatoes into the boiling water, return the water to a boil, adjust the heat to maintain a steady simmer, and cook until a knife inserted into a potato meets no resistance, 25 to 30 minutes.

2. Drain the potatoes into a colander and let cool just until they can be handled, then peel them. Pass the warm potatoes through a ricer held over a large bowl, or place the potatoes in the bowl and mash with a potato masher until smooth. Set aside.

3. In a medium sauté pan, melt the butter over medium-high heat. Add the onion and garlic and cook, stirring occasionally, until the onion is translucent, about 4 minutes. Add the spinach and cook, stirring occasionally, until wilted, about 3 minutes. Add the sauerkraut and stir to mix well. Remove the pan from the heat.

4. Add the spinach-sauerkraut mixture to the potatoes and mix well, then stir in 1 tsp salt and the Parmesan cheese. Let cool completely.

5. *To make the dough,* in a stand mixer fitted with the paddle attachment, mix together the all-purpose flour and rye flour on low speed. Add the eggs, ½ cup/120 ml water, and canola oil. Continue to mix on low speed for 1 minute, and then increase the speed to medium and mix until the dough comes together, 2 to 3 minutes. Increase the mixer speed by one setting and continue mixing until all of the ingredients are thoroughly combined and a tight dough ball has formed, about 5 minutes.

6. Remove the dough from the bowl, wrap in plastic wrap, and let sit at room temperature for 1 hour. (The dough can also be wrapped and refrigerated overnight; bring to room temperature before continuing.)

7. Have ready a small bowl of warm water. Lightly flour a work surface. Unwrap the dough and cut it into six equal portions. Place one portion on the floured work surface and roll out ⅛ in/3 mm thick. Using a round cookie cutter

about 4½ in/11 cm in diameter, cut out as many rounds as possible. Spoon about 1½ tbsp of the filling onto the center of a round. Using a fingertip, dampen the edges of the round, then fold over to enclose the filling, forming a half-moon, and press the edges firmly to seal. Repeat until all of the dough portions and filling are used.

8. Fill a large pot three-fourths full with water, season the water with enough salt to make it almost as salty as seawater, and bring to a boil over high heat. Drop in the dumplings, stir to prevent them from sticking together, and cook until tender, 6 to 7 minutes. Using a slotted spoon, transfer them to a sheet pan and toss them with a little oil to prevent them from sticking together.

9. In a large frying pan, heat 1½ tbsp canola oil over medium-high heat. Working in batches, add the dumplings in a single layer and cook, turning once, until golden brown on both sides, about 4 minutes on each side. Using a slotted spoon, transfer the dumplings to a platter and keep warm. Repeat with the remaining dumplings, adding more oil as needed to prevent sticking.

10. When all of the dumplings have been browned, melt the butter in the pan over medium heat. When the butter turns amber brown and releases a nutty aroma, remove it from the heat and pour it over the dumplings.

11. Serve the dumplings immediately. Pass the sour cream at the table.

SPINACH-AND-POTATO-STUFFED PASTA
WITH CHANTERELLE MUSHROOMS
GRATINIERTE MAULTASCHEN

JEREMY LEARNED HOW TO MAKE *MAULTASCHEN,* the German version of ravioli, working at the Liederkranz restaurant in Reading. The women in the kitchen had a unique stuffing technique: they spooned the filling in an even horizontal line near the bottom of a full sheet of semolina pasta, folded the edge of the sheet over the line of filling, spooned a second line of filling in the immediate crevice, and then folded it over, creating two distinct, evenly sealed rows that were then cut crosswise into squares. This method helps us to bang out generously and uniformly stuffed pasta at the restaurant. The filling here is vegetarian but extremely robust. It makes a nice side but can also be a satisfying main course.

INGREDIENTS (SERVES 4 TO 6)

FILLING

Kosher salt

1 lb/455 g Yukon gold potatoes

1 tbsp unsalted butter

1 yellow onion, finely chopped

2 garlic cloves, minced

6 oz/170 g spinach, chopped

DOUGH

1½ cups/210 g all-purpose flour, plus more for dusting

3 eggs, lightly beaten

2 tbsp water

Kosher salt

1 cup/240 ml heavy cream

8 oz/225 g chanterelle or oyster mushrooms

6 sprigs fresh thyme

1. *To make the filling,* fill a medium pot two-thirds full with water, add enough salt for the water to taste like seawater, and bring to a boil over high heat. Slip the potatoes into the boiling water, return the water to a boil, adjust the heat to maintain a steady simmer, and cook until a knife inserted into a potato meets no resistance, 25 to 30 minutes.

2. Drain the potatoes into a colander and let cool just until they can be handled, then peel them.

Pass the warm potatoes through a ricer held over a large bowl, or place the potatoes in the bowl and mash with a potato masher until smooth. Let cool completely.

3. In a medium sauté pan, melt the butter over medium-high heat. Add the onion, garlic, and 1 tsp salt and cook, stirring occasionally, until the onion is translucent, about 4 minutes. Add the spinach and cook, stirring occasionally, until wilted, about 3 minutes. Remove the pan from the heat, add the spinach mixture to the potatoes, and mix well. Set aside.

4. *To make the dough,* in a stand mixer fitted with the paddle attachment, combine the flour, eggs, and 2 tbsp water and mix on low speed for 1 minute. Increase the speed to medium and mix until the dough comes together, 2 to 3 minutes. Increase the mixer speed by one setting and continue mixing until all of the ingredients are thoroughly combined and a tight dough ball forms, about 5 minutes.

5. Remove the dough from the bowl, wrap in plastic wrap, and let sit at room temperature for 1 hour. (The dough can also be wrapped and refrigerated overnight; bring to room temperature before continuing.)

6. Lightly flour a work surface. Unwrap the dough and cut it into four equal portions. Place one portion on the floured work surface and roll out into a thin sheet about 12 in/30.5 cm long and 5 in/12 cm wide. (Alternatively, following the manufacturer's instructions, roll out the dough on a pasta machine.) Lightly dust a kitchen towel with flour, transfer the pasta sheet to the towel, and then lightly dust the pasta sheet. Repeat with the remaining dough portions.

7. Clean the work surface and then dust again with flour. Have ready a small bowl of warm water. Lay a dough sheet, with a long side facing you, on the floured surface. Working about 1 in/ 2.5 cm from the edge nearest you, spoon the filling in a row the length of the sheet, stopping just short of both ends. Lift the edge nearest you over the filling, covering it completely. Now, spoon a second row of filling next to the edge of the folded dough sheet. Fold the dough over again away from you, covering the second row of filling

completely. Using a fingertip, dampen the entire perimeter of the sheet with a little warm water. Fold the dough over one last time and press the edges to seal. You should have a large stuffed pasta with two individual rows of filling. Using the tapered end of a French rolling pin, the back of a narrow wooden spoon, or other similar-size surface, push down firmly on the stuffed pasta at 2-in/5-cm intervals, creating stuffed "pockets." Now, using a paring knife, cut between the pockets, then press down on the cut edge of each pocket to seal it closed. Set the Maultaschen aside on a floured sheet pan or kitchen towel. Repeat with the remaining dough sheets and filling until all of the filling is used.

8. Preheat the oven to 350°F/180°C. Fill a large pot three-fourths full with water, season the water with enough salt to make it almost as salty as seawater, and bring to a boil over high heat. Drop in the Maultaschen, stir to prevent them from sticking together, adjust the heat to maintain a gentle boil, and cook until tender, 6 to 7 minutes. Using a slotted spoon, transfer them to a 9-by-12-in/23-by-30.5-cm or similar-size baking dish. (If you will not be baking the Maultaschen right away, transfer them to a sheet pan and toss them with a little oil to prevent them from sticking together.

9. Pour the cream evenly over the top. If using chanterelles, trim the stem ends; if using oyster mushrooms, pull the clusters apart into bite-size pieces and trim the stem ends. Distribute the thyme sprigs evenly around the pasta and scatter the mushrooms evenly over the top.

10. Bake until the cream starts to brown and the mushrooms are tender, about 30 minutes. Serve immediately.

BUTTERNUT SQUASH-STUFFED PASTA
WITH CHESTNUT AND SAGE BROWN BUTTER
KÜRBIS MAULTASCHEN

THIS DISH is made the same way as Spinach-and-Potato-Stuffed Pasta with Chanterelle Mushrooms (page 180), but here the pasta is filled with butternut squash and cheese and is topped with an autumnal-inspired mix of chestnuts, sage, and brown butter. Serve alongside a roast or braised meat or on its own as a vegetarian main course.

INGREDIENTS (SERVES 4 TO 6)

FILLING

1 tbsp canola oil

1 tbsp unsalted butter

1 lb/455 g butternut or kabocha squash, cut into ½-in/12-mm cubes

1 yellow onion, finely chopped

2 garlic cloves, minced

1 tsp kosher salt

½ cup/55 g grated aged Gouda or Prima Donna cheese

DOUGH

1½ cups/210 g all-purpose flour, plus more for dusting

3 eggs, lightly beaten

2 tbsp water

Kosher salt

Canola or grapeseed oil for tossing and browning the pasta

½ cup/115 g unsalted butter

10 to 12 vacuum-sealed or jarred peeled chestnuts, crushed

6 fresh sage leaves

¼ cup/60 ml fresh lemon juice

1. *To make the filling,* in a medium frying pan, heat the canola oil and butter over medium-high heat. Add the squash and cook, stirring often, until lightly browned, about 8 minutes. Turn the heat to low; add the onion, garlic, and salt; and cook slowly, stirring occasionally, until the squash is tender, about 10 minutes.

2. Remove the pan from the heat and transfer the squash mixture to a medium bowl. Using a potato masher or a wooden spoon, mash the squash until smooth. Add the cheese and mix well. Set aside to cool completely.

(Continued)

3. *To make the dough,* in a stand mixer fitted with the paddle attachment, combine the flour, eggs, and water and mix on low speed for 1 minute. Increase the speed to medium and mix until the dough comes together, 2 to 3 minutes. Increase the mixer speed by one setting and continue mixing until all of the ingredients are thoroughly combined and a tight dough ball forms, about 5 minutes.

4. Remove the dough from the bowl, wrap in plastic wrap, and let sit at room temperature for 1 hour. (The dough can also be wrapped and refrigerated overnight; bring to room temperature before continuing.)

5. Lightly flour a work surface. Unwrap the dough and cut it into four equal portions. Place one portion on the floured work surface and roll out into a thin sheet about 12 in/30.5 cm long and 5 in/12 cm wide. (Alternatively, following the manufacturer's instructions, roll out the dough on a pasta machine.) Lightly dust a kitchen towel with flour, transfer the pasta sheet to the towel, and then lightly dust the pasta sheet. Repeat with the remaining dough portions.

6. Clean the work surface and then dust again with flour. Have ready a small bowl of warm water. Lay a dough sheet, with a long side facing you, on the floured surface. Working about 1 in/ 2.5 cm from the edge nearest you, spoon the filling in a row the length of the sheet, stopping just short of both ends. Lift the edge near you over the filling, covering it completely. Now, spoon a second row of filling next to the edge of the folded dough sheet. Fold the dough over again away from you, covering the second row of filling completely. Using a fingertip, dampen the entire perimeter of the sheet with a little warm water. Fold the dough over one last time

and press the edges to seal. You should have a large stuffed pasta with two individual rows of filling. Using the tapered end of a French rolling pin, the back of a narrow wooden spoon, or other similar-size surface, push down firmly on the stuffed pasta at 2-in/5-cm intervals, creating stuffed "pockets." Now, using a paring knife, cut between the pockets, then press down on the cut edge of each pocket to seal it closed. Set the Maultaschen aside on a floured sheet pan or kitchen towel. Repeat with the remaining dough sheets and filling until all of the filling is used.

7. Fill a large pot three-fourths full with water, season the water with enough salt to make it almost as salty as seawater, and bring to a boil over high heat. Drop in the Maultaschen, stir to prevent them from sticking together, adjust the heat to maintain a gentle boil, and cook until tender, 6 to 7 minutes. Using a slotted spoon, transfer them to a sheet pan and toss them with a little oil to prevent them from sticking together.

8. In a large frying pan, heat 1½ tbsp canola oil over medium-high heat. Working in batches, add the Maultaschen in a single layer and cook, turning once, until golden brown on both sides, about 4 minutes on each side. Using a slotted spoon, transfer the Maultaschen to a platter and keep warm. Repeat with the remaining Maultaschen, adding more oil as needed to prevent sticking.

9. When all of the pasta has been browned, melt the butter in the pan over medium heat. When the butter turns amber brown and releases a nutty aroma, add the chestnuts and sage and stir until the chestnuts are heated through. Whisk in the lemon juice, then pour the brown butter sauce over the Maultaschen and serve immediately.

PICKLES & CONDIMENTS

EINGELEGTES GEMÜSE

IN GERMANY AND BEYOND, the interest in pickling and other types of preserving has grown dramatically in recent years. Before the advent of refrigeration, these practices were critical to survival. Nowadays, they are a way to hold on to the tastes and traditions of the past.

The techniques and flavors behind pickling have changed little over the years. Sauerkraut, the most celebrated of all of Germany's brined specialties, is made essentially the same way today as it has been for centuries. Differences in taste on the brine spectrum exist among countries, however. The pickles of Germany are less sweet than those of Scandinavia and eastern Europe and are sweeter than most of the sour, salty styles popular in the United States.

Thanks to the presence of the Amish and the Pennsylvania Dutch, Philadelphia offers a rich choice of pickled foods. Stop in at the city's landmark Reading Terminal Market and, just a few booths down from our Wursthaus Schmitz stand, you'll find a wonderland of pickled items, with deli cases, jars, and platters displaying every vegetable imaginable. We don't presume to turn out better pickles than these professional pickle makers, but there is plenty in this chapter to tempt those who crave good pickles of many different kinds. We have also included a pair of spicy, robust mustards for accompanying sausages and other cured meats, for spreading on sandwiches, and for dressing up Brotzeit platters.

MUSTARD PICKLES
SENFGURKEN

THE CUCUMBERS FOR THESE PICKLES, featuring the assertive characteristics of both mustard seeds and dry mustard, should be cut in half-moons rather than chips or spears. This is the traditional cut for this pickle, which is a popular addition to cheese plates, charcuterie spreads, or a Brotzeit platter.

INGREDIENTS (MAKES ABOUT I QT/260 G)

2 cups/480 ml cider vinegar

1 cup/240 ml water

2 tbsp kosher salt

1 tbsp sugar

1 tsp ground turmeric

1 tbsp Colman's dry mustard

1 tbsp yellow mustard seeds

1 tsp dill seeds

4 Kirby or 2 large English cucumbers, peeled, halved lengthwise, seeded, and cut crosswise into half-moons ½ in/12 mm thick

1. In a medium saucepan, combine the vinegar, water, salt, sugar, turmeric, dry mustard, mustard seeds, and dill seeds and bring to a boil over high heat. Remove the pan from the heat and let the mixture cool to room temperature.

2. Put the cucumbers in a nonreactive container large enough to hold them and the liquid, then pour the cooled liquid over the cucumbers, submerging them. Cover and refrigerate.

3. The pickles will be ready after about 3 days. They will keep in the refrigerator for up to 2 weeks.

PICKLED RED BEETS AND EGGS

ROTE BETE UND EIER

YOU CAN FIND PICKLED EGGS everywhere in Germany, but they are most frequently made with a salt brine rather than a vinegar one. The addition of beets here is a shout-out to Berks County where Jeremy grew up. Most local bars have big jars of red-stained pickled eggs at the ready for any drinker craving a quick beer snack. The pickling process here is longer than it is for most of the recipes in this chapter, and it results in eggs that will last for about 6 weeks in the fridge.

INGREDIENTS (MAKES ABOUT 3 QT/270 G)

1 lb/455 g red beets, peeled

1½ cups/360 ml red wine vinegar, plus more if needed

1½ cups/360 ml red wine

1½ tbsp kosher salt

1½ tbsp sugar

2 tsp black peppercorns

1 tsp whole cloves

2 fresh bay leaves, or 1 dried bay leaf

3 star anise pods

1 red onion, sliced

12 hard-boiled eggs, peeled

1. In a large saucepan, combine the beets with water to cover and bring to a boil over high heat. Cook the beets until they are tender when pierced in the center with a paring knife, 30 minutes to 1 hour, depending on their size.

2. Scoop out the beets and set aside to cool, then cover and refrigerate overnight. Measure 2½ cups/600 ml of the beet cooking liquid and reserve. Discard the remaining cooking liquid or reserve for another use.

3. Pour the reserved beet liquid into a medium saucepan and add the vinegar, wine, salt, sugar, peppercorns, cloves, bay leaves, and star anise and bring to a boil over high heat. Remove the pan from the heat, let the liquid cool, transfer to a covered container, and refrigerate overnight.

4. The next day, slice the beets ½ in/12 mm thick. Divide the beets, onion, and eggs evenly among three 1-qt/960-ml jars (or equivalent capacity) and pour in the chilled beet liquid mixture to cover. If the liquid does not cover the vegetables and eggs, add vinegar as needed to cover. Cover and refrigerate.

5. The pickled vegetables and eggs will be ready in 4 days. They will keep in the refrigerator for up to 6 weeks.

PICKLED MIXED VEGETABLES
EINGELEGTES GEMÜSE

AS A KID, Jeremy and his family often went for dinner at the Alpenhof, a German inn in Reading that is now sadly closed. One of his best memories of the place was the pickle bowl that would appear as soon you sat down: a monkey dish brimming with a mix of cauliflower, carrots, pearl onions, peppers, cucumbers, and more. This mixed-vegetable pickle, which shares style points with Italian *giardiniera,* can work as an Alpenhof-style starter on its own or with cold meats and cheese spreads for Brotzeit.

INGREDIENTS (MAKES ABOUT 3 QT/2.8 L)

6 cups/1.4 L water

6 cups/1.4 L white vinegar

4 cups/960 ml cider vinegar

½ cup/95 g kosher salt

3 garlic cloves, minced

1 tbsp coriander seeds

1 tbsp dill seeds

1 tbsp yellow mustard seeds

1 tbsp sugar

1 tsp black peppercorns

½ tsp red pepper flakes

¼ tsp ground turmeric

2 fresh bay leaves

1 cauliflower, cored and divided into small florets

1 carrot, peeled and sliced ½ in/12 mm thick

12 pearl onions, peeled

2 Kirby cucumbers, sliced ½ in/12 mm thick

1 red bell pepper, seeded and sliced lengthwise ½ in/12 mm wide

1 green bell pepper, seeded and sliced lengthwise ½ in/12 mm wide

1. In a medium stockpot, combine the water, white and cider vinegars, salt, garlic, coriander seeds, dill seeds, mustard seeds, sugar, peppercorns, red pepper flakes, turmeric, and bay leaves and bring to a boil over high heat. Remove the pot from the heat.

2. Place the cauliflower, carrot, and onions in a heatproof container large enough to accommodate them and the brine and pour the hot brine over them. Place a plate on top of the mixture, put a weight on the plate so the vegetables stay submerged, let cool to room temperature, cover the container, and refrigerate overnight.

3. The next day, add the cucumbers and both bell peppers to the container and return it to the refrigerator. The pickles will be ready in 1 week. They will keep in the refrigerator for up to 6 weeks.

PICKLED SAUSAGES
PÖKELWURST

ALL OF THE OLD-TIMEY BARS in Berks County stock jars of what they call "hot bologna," spicy pickled sausages that are doled out to drinkers in a manner similar to German *Landjäger*, the semidried beef sausages enjoyed throughout southern Germany. To pickle your own sausages, look for a cured, smoked pork sausage about the diameter of a hot dog. If you can find German frankfurters or even Landjäger sausages, they would work fine here, as would long, smoky Polish *kabanos*.

INGREDIENTS (MAKES ABOUT 2 LB/910 G)

2 cups/480 ml water

2 cups/480 ml white wine vinegar

4 garlic cloves, minced

2 tbsp kosher salt

1 tbsp yellow mustard seeds

1 tsp red pepper flakes

½ tsp whole allspice

2 fresh bay leaves, or 1 dried bay leaf

2 lb/910 g cured, smoked sausages, cut into slices ½ in/12 mm thick

1. In a medium saucepan, combine the water, vinegar, garlic, salt, mustard seeds, red pepper flakes, allspice, and bay leaves and bring to a boil over high heat. Remove the pan from the heat.

2. Put the sausages in a heatproof container large enough to accommodate them and the brine and pour the hot brine over them. Let cool to room temperature, then cover and refrigerate.

3. The sausages will be ready in 3 days. They will keep in the refrigerator for up to 4 weeks.

NATURALLY FERMENTED SAUERKRAUT

SAUERKRAUT

SAUERKRAUT is slightly misplaced in this chapter, as it's not made with vinegar. The preserving process is reliant on nothing more than cabbage, salt, and microorganisms that work to produce the lactic acid that creates the sour flavor profile. As simplistic as this sounds, this recipe is unlike any sauerkraut you will buy off the store shelf. It has a much more natural, unvarnished taste, and the lack of commercial additives means its digestive and probiotic qualities are delivered even more directly. The trickiest part is acquiring the proper container. You need a setup that doesn't allow air in but lets CO_2 escape. A 1-gl/4-L food-grade plastic bucket, glass jar, or stoneware crock; a plate that fits inside the rim of the container; a smaller glass jar filled with water to use as a weight; and a loose-fitting lid is the best option.

NOTE: *Using percentages is the best way to measure the salt for this recipe. It needs to be 2.5 percent of the weight of the shredded cabbage. Using this method, you can use any size cabbage you want. Just take the total weight of the cabbage and multiply it by 0.025. That's the amount of salt you'll need to ferment your cabbage.*

INGREDIENTS (MAKES 4 QT/3 KG)

2 medium heads green cabbage, about 3¼ lb/1.5 kg total weight

Kosher salt (2.5 percent total weight of cabbage)

2 fresh bay leaves, or 1 dried bay leaf

10 juniper berries

1. Remove the outer leaves from the cabbage heads to ensure there are no blemishes. Usually you need to remove only the first one or two layers. Cut each head in half through the stem end, then cut the halves lengthwise in half again. Using a small, sharp knife, remove the hard core from each cabbage quarter. Using a food processor fitted with the grater attachment or a large, sharp knife, thinly shred the cabbage quarters crosswise.

2. Put the cabbage in a large bowl. Measure the salt. If you have started with 2 medium cabbage heads, you will need about 3 tbsp/35 g. Use the formula provided in the Note to determine the correct amount. Add the salt, bay leaves, and juniper berries to the cabbage and mix well with your hands, massaging the salt into the cabbage so that the cabbage starts to release liquid. You want it to release a lot of liquid in the first 24 hours.

3. When the cabbage is well mixed with the spices, pack it into your fermenting container as tightly as possible: put a little of the cabbage in the bottom, use a potato masher to flatten it, add more cabbage and flatten again, and continue in this manner until all of the cabbage is tightly packed in the container. Then pour the liquid remaining in the bowl into the container.

4. Topping the cabbage with a weight helps draw out water and create a brine, keeping the cabbage safe from unwanted bacteria. At Brauhaus Schmitz, we typically use a stoneware crock and a stone weight, but a lidded canning jar filled with water works fine. If using a stone weight, place it directly on the cabbage and push down hard. If using a water-filled jar, put a plate on top of the cabbage and place the jar on top of the plate.

5. If the fermenting container is plastic, place the lid on but keep it a little loose. If you are using an airlocked container, tighten the lid and fill the airlock with water. The crock we use is equipped with a channel that you fill with water, which prevents air from getting in yet allows gas to escape. You don't want constant air, because the oxygen will encourage unwanted bacteria that can spoil your kraut.

6. Place the container in a cool, dark place for 24 hours. At the end of that time, check to see if a brine has formed and the cabbage is submerged in liquid. (If not, mix together water and salt in a ratio of 1 cup/240 ml water to 1 tsp kosher salt and add it as needed to submerge the cabbage.)

7. Once the cabbage is covered with brine, place it in a cool, dark spot and let it ferment. This will take anywhere from 2 to 4 weeks. Check on it daily to see how it's doing. You will know that it has begun to ferment when you see tiny bubbles forming around the edge of plate holding the weight. Sometimes a little bit of mold or scum will form on top; just lift it off with a ladle and let the cabbage continue to ferment. After 1 week, check to see how it is doing. The bubbles should be more visible. After about 2 weeks, the cabbage should begin to smell like sauerkraut. Try a little; if it has a nice sour taste, it is ready. If it is not yet sour enough, leave it to ferment longer.

8. When the sauerkraut is ready, transfer it to smaller containers and refrigerate. It will keep for up to 1 month.

SWEET AND SPICY BEER MUSTARD

BIERSENF

THIS RECIPE, which was featured in *Food & Wine* magazine, marries Jeremy's love of cooking with beer with the most essential condiment of the German table. Typical German mustards don't contain alcohol, but the addition of a dark beer, such as a double-bock lager from southern Germany, creates a malty profile here that is particularly enjoyable.

INGREDIENTS (MAKES 1 QT/960 ML)

½ cup/110 g black mustard seeds

½ cup/110 g yellow mustard seeds

1½ cups/360 ml malt vinegar

2 cups/480 ml dark beer

5 tbsp/100 g honey

½ cup/110 g firmly packed dark brown sugar

2 tsp kosher salt

2 tsp ground allspice

¾ tsp ground turmeric

1 cup/100 g Colman's dry mustard

1. In a medium bowl, combine the black and yellow mustard seeds, vinegar, and 1½ cups/ 360 ml of the beer and stir well. Cover and refrigerate overnight.

2. In a medium saucepan, combine the remaining ½ cup/120 ml beer with the honey, brown sugar, salt, allspice, and turmeric and bring to a boil over medium-high heat, stirring to dissolve the sugar. Boil until reduced by half, about 15 minutes.

3. Remove the pan from the heat and let cool to room temperature. Transfer to a blender, add the dry mustard and the mustard-seed mixture, and process on medium speed until thoroughly combined but still a bit chunky, about 2 minutes.

4. Transfer the mustard to a glass jar, cover, and refrigerate overnight before serving. The mustard will keep in the refrigerator for up to 3 months.

PILSNER HORSERADISH MUSTARD

MEERRETTICH SENF

UNLIKE THE WHOLE-GRAIN MUSTARD on the facing page, this is a smooth yellow mustard that is heavy on horseradish, which adds an appealingly nasal kick of spice that slices through fattier meat preparations. Consider the popular Jever brand for the pilsner here, or you can even substitute a hoppy IPA.

INGREDIENTS (MAKES 1 QT/960 ML)

2 cups/480 ml cider vinegar

1 cup/240 ml pilsner beer

2 tbsp kosher salt

2 tbsp sugar

1 tsp ground turmeric

½ cup/50 g Colman's dry mustard

1 cup/220 g yellow mustard seeds

½ cup/120 g freshly grated or prepared horseradish

1. In a medium saucepan, combine the vinegar, beer, salt, and sugar and bring to a boil over high heat, stirring to dissolve the sugar. Turn the heat to low, add the turmeric, and simmer for 15 minutes to blend the flavors.

2. Remove the pan from the heat and let cool to room temperature. Transfer to a blender, add the dry mustard, mustard seeds, and horseradish, and process until thoroughly combined and smooth, about 3 minutes. If you prefer more texture, process for a shorter time.

3. Transfer the mustard to a glass jar, cover, and refrigerate overnight before serving. The mustard will keep in the refrigerator for up to 3 months.

9

DESSERTS

NACHTISCH

GERMAN DESSERTS are hindered by the same faulty generalizations that afflict their savory counterparts in the kitchen. Everything's heavy, clunky, roly-poly, and soaked in insane amounts of butter, right? Not even close. There's so much more to the sweet side of this tradition, and it has long been Jessica's objective to meld Germany's baking and pastry heritage with her own ideas as gracefully as possible.

But before we delve more deeply into the dessert offerings at Brauhaus Schmitz, we must answer a question that is regularly asked at the restaurant: No, German chocolate cake is *not* German! The choco-coconut-pecan sugar bomb is a 100 percent American invention, named for Sam German, the guy who developed the commercially available baker's chocolate originally used for this Betty Crocker special. However, two other desserts widely recognized as being German by Americans, apple strudel (see page 210) and Black Forest cake, are indeed just that. But there is much more to the German dessert repertoire than these two classics. Many contemporary desserts and dessert techniques that Americans often associate with French or Italian bakers have their roots with German and Austrian pastry traditions. At Brauhaus Schmitz, we strive to honor this legacy while embracing contemporary touches.

Our selections also respect both seasonality and restraint. Indeed, the simplicity of everyday desserts in Germany is inspiring. Germans often approach a bowl of fresh berries topped with whipped cream with the same excitement that American dessert lovers express for a triple hot fudge caramel brownie. At Brauhaus Schmitz, our desserts favor the simpler side of the dessert equation, allowing the ingredients, manipulated in the right ways at the right times of year, to speak for themselves.

Many of these recipes, much more so than their savory counterparts, require precision to achieve the best possible results. Because of this, we recommend using a digital scale and following the gram measurements for the baking recipes.

GINGERBREAD COOKIES WITH ORANGE GLAZE

LEBKUCHEN

COOKIES are a German baking obsession, and there's no time of year during which this is more apparent than the winter holidays. We use a relatively standard gingerbread formula for *Lebkuchen*, but we deliberately underbake them so the center stays a little sticky, which helps the candied citrus stand out that much more.

INGREDIENTS (MAKES ABOUT TWENTY-FOUR 4-IN/10-CM COOKIES)

⅓ cup/110 g honey

¾ cup/250 g unsulfured molasses

4 cups/560 g all-purpose flour, plus more for dusting

1 tsp baking soda

¼ tsp kosher salt

¾ cup/170 g unsalted butter, at room temperature, plus more for preparing the pan

¼ cup/55 g firmly packed brown sugar

1½ tbsp Spice Mix (page 212)

1 tsp grated orange zest

1 tsp chopped candied lemon

2 eggs

GLAZE

2 cups/240 g confectioners' sugar

Grated zest of 1 orange, plus 2 tbsp fresh orange juice

½ tsp vanilla extract

¼ tsp kosher salt

1. In a small saucepan, combine the honey and molasses over high heat and bring to a boil. Remove from the heat and let cool for 10 minutes.

2. Meanwhile, in a medium bowl, sift together the flour, baking soda, and salt and set aside. In a stand mixer fitted with the paddle attachment, beat together the butter and brown sugar on medium speed until light and fluffy, about 5 minutes.

3. Add the spice mix, orange zest, and candied lemon to the cooled honey mixture, stir well, then pour the mixture into the butter-sugar

mixture. On low speed, beat until well combined, about 2 minutes. Scrape down the sides of the bowl, add the eggs, and beat on medium speed until well mixed.

4. On low speed, add the flour mixture to the butter mixture and beat until a soft and sticky but not runny dough forms. (If necessary, add more flour, a spoonful at a time, to achieve a good consistency.) Pour the dough into a container, cover tightly, and refrigerate overnight.

5. The next day, preheat the oven to 350°F/ 180°C. Butter a large sheet pan.

(Continued)

6. Scoop the dough into golf-ball-size balls and place on the prepared sheet pan, spacing them about 2 in/5 cm apart.

7. Bake the cookies until they are evenly golden but remain slightly gooey in the center, 10 to 15 minutes. Transfer to a cooling rack and let cool completely.

8. *To make the glaze,* in a small bowl, combine the confectioners' sugar, orange zest, orange juice, vanilla, and salt and stir well until a thick, free-flowing glaze forms.

9. Spoon about 1 tbsp of the glaze onto the top of each cookie. Let dry at room temperature for about 30 minutes before serving. Store leftover cookies in an airtight container at room temperature for up to 4 days.

ANISEED SUGAR COOKIES
SPRINGERLE

A TRADITIONAL GERMAN CONFECTION, these cookies are more like a biscuit than a cookie: they contain no butter and are crunchy and a bit dry rather than moist and chewy. They're also best eaten the day you make them. The most distinguishing characteristics of *Springerle*, aside from their robust anise flavor, are the designs embossed into them, which are achieved with either specially designed molds or carved rolling pins. At the restaurant, we have a special hand-carved pin lined with beautiful, intricate nature scenes that transfer to the dough on careful rolling. The best place to look for these tools is at specialty kitchen stores or online. Fante's Kitchen Shop, a favorite of ours in Philadelphia, has an excellent website (www.fantes.com).

INGREDIENTS (MAKES ABOUT 48 COOKIES)

Nonstick cooking spray for preparing the pan

1½ tbsp crushed aniseeds

3½ cups/490 g all-purpose flour, plus more for dusting

1 tsp baking powder

4 eggs

2 cups/400 g granulated sugar

½ tsp vanilla extract

¼ cup/30 g confectioners' sugar

1. Coat a large sheet pan with nonstick cooking spray, sprinkle evenly with the aniseeds, and set aside.

2. In a bowl, stir together the flour and baking powder and set aside. In a stand mixer fitted with the paddle attachment, beat together the eggs, granulated sugar, and vanilla on medium speed until frothy, about 5 minutes. Remove the bowl from the mixer stand and slowly stir in the flour mixture until a thick, soft, moist dough forms, about 2 minutes.

3. On a lightly floured work surface, roll out the dough ¼ in/6 mm thick. Sift a light layer of the confectioners' sugar over the dough.

4. *If using a Springerle mold,* lightly dust the mold with flour, tapping off the excess, then gently press the mold into the dough until the design has been clearly transferred. Constant, even pressure must be used to transfer the design. Do not push too hard or the cookies will be uneven. Lift the mold, cut around each design with a small knife, and transfer the cookies to the prepared sheet pan.

If using a Springerle pin, lightly dust the pin with flour, tapping off the excess, and slowly and firmly roll it over the dough. Cut around each design with a small knife and transfer the cookies to the prepared sheet pan. (If you find that a clear design has not been transferred, you can gather up the dough, reknead it briefly, and roll it out again.)

(Continued)

5. Cover the cookies with a clean kitchen towel and let dry at room temperature for at least 8 hours or preferably overnight. As the cookies dry, the seeds will stick to the dough.

6. The next day, preheat the oven to 250°F/ 120°C.

7. Bake the cookies until the tops are pale brown, about 10 minutes. Let the cookies cool on the pan on a wire rack.

8. For the best texture and flavor, eat the cookies the same day they are baked. Store leftover cookies in an airtight container at room temperature and eat them as soon as possible.

PUMPERNICKEL BROWNIES
SCHOKO SCHNITTEN

WHILE STORE-BOUGHT PUMPERNICKEL is regarded as a sacrilege by most German bread purists, it ended up being the right move for this recipe. The gooey, chocolatey brownies are made infinitely chewier by the addition of finely pulsed toasted bread. Homemade pumpernickel, which is wonderfully dense due to its long bake time, is ideal in almost all situations, except here, where it proves too "rubbery" for these tasty snacks.

INGREDIENTS (MAKES SIXTEEN 2-IN/5-CM BROWNIES)

Butter for preparing the baking dish, plus ½ cup/ 115 g unsalted butter

4 slices pumpernickel bread, torn into small pieces

2¼ cups/450 g sugar

2 tbsp brewed coffee

1¼ cups/110 g Dutch-processed cocoa powder

1 tsp baking powder

4 eggs

1½ tsp kosher salt

1 tbsp vanilla extract

1½ cups/210 g all-purpose flour

1 cup/170 g semisweet chocolate chips

1. Preheat the oven to 375°F/190°C and butter an 8-in/20-cm square baking dish. Spread the pumpernickel pieces on a sheet pan and toast in the oven until they have crisped slightly, about 15 minutes. Remove from the oven and set aside to cool, then crush into coarse crumbs. Turn the oven temperature to 350°F/180°C.

2. In a medium saucepan, melt the ½ cup/ 115 g butter with the sugar and coffee over medium heat, then simmer, stirring, just until the sugar dissolves. Remove from the heat and let cool slightly.

3. In a medium bowl, whisk together the butter mixture, cocoa powder, baking powder, eggs, salt, and vanilla until smooth. Add the flour and stir until incorporated. Stir in the chocolate chips and three-fourths of the pumpernickel crumbs.

4. Pour the batter into the prepared baking dish and scatter the remaining pumpernickel crumbs evenly over the top. Bake until just set and a cake tester or a toothpick inserted into the center comes out a little wet, about 30 minutes. Let cool in the dish on a wire rack for 30 minutes, then cut into 2-in/5-cm squares and remove from the dish.

5. Serve the brownies warm or at room temperature. Store leftover brownies in an airtight container at room temperature for up to 5 days.

CHERRY AND QUARK CHEESE STRUDEL

KIRSCHSTRUDEL

THIS IS ONE OF THE FIRST DESSERT SPECIALS WE OFFERED at the restaurant, and it has remained so popular that we also offered it during our visit to the James Beard House in 2012. Quark cheese is used for a number of savory German preparations, such as our herbed dumplings on page 174, but it is an important dessert ingredient, as well. It's the ideal creamy counterpart to this strudel's cherry filling (try it with fresh fruit for an easy dessert), flavored with orange juice and zest, cinnamon, and vanilla.

INGREDIENTS (SERVES 8)

CHEESE FILLING

12 oz/340 g quark or farmer cheese, at room temperature

12 oz/340 g cream cheese, at room temperature

½ cup/100 g granulated sugar

2 tbsp cornstarch

½ tsp kosher salt

CHERRY FILLING

8 oz/225 g frozen or pitted fresh cherries

Grated zest and juice of ½ orange

Grated zest and juice of ½ lemon

1 cinnamon stick

½ cup/100 g granulated sugar

2 tsp kosher salt

½ vanilla bean

2 tbsp cornstarch

2 tbsp water

One 1-lb/455-g box phyllo dough, thawed if frozen and at room temperature

1 cup/225 g unsalted butter, melted

Confectioners' sugar for dusting (optional)

1. *To make the cheese filling,* in a stand mixer fitted with the paddle attachment, combine the quark, cream cheese, granulated sugar, cornstarch, and salt and beat on medium speed until completely smooth, 5 to 7 minutes. Pour the mixture into a clean bowl, cover with plastic wrap, and refrigerate overnight.

2. *To make the cherry filling,* in a saucepan, combine the cherries, orange zest and juice, lemon zest and juice, cinnamon stick, granulated sugar, and salt. Split the vanilla bean in half lengthwise, then, using the tip of the knife, scrape the seeds from the halves into the cherry mixture. Place the pan over medium heat and bring the mixture to a boil, stirring until the sugar dissolves. Adjust the heat to maintain a simmer and cook for 10 minutes. Remove from the heat and let steep for 30 minutes.

3. In a small bowl, stir together the cornstarch and water until the cornstarch has dissolved. Return the cherry mixture to medium heat, bring to a simmer, and stir in the cornstarch slurry. Cook, stirring constantly, until the mixture comes to a boil and thickens. Remove from the heat, pour into a heatproof container, let cool completely, cover, and refrigerate overnight.

4. Preheat the oven to 375°F/190°C. Line a sheet pan with parchment paper.

5. Unroll the stack of phyllo dough on a clean work surface. Remove one sheet from the stack, lay it on the parchment-lined pan, and brush it lightly with melted butter. Continue stacking the sheets on the parchment, brushing each one lightly with butter, until you have 15 layers. Reserve any remaining phyllo sheets for another use. (When you are not removing sheets from the stack, keep the stack covered with plastic wrap to prevent the sheets from drying out.)

6. Position the sheet pan so a long side of the phyllo sheets is facing you. Spread the cheese mixture onto the layered phyllo, leaving a ½-in/ 12-mm border uncovered on all four sides. Spoon the cherries evenly onto the cheese. Starting from the long side facing you, roll up the layered phyllo away from you, folding in the sides as you roll. Don't worry if some of the cheese or cherry filling leaks out. Position the roll, seam-side down, in the center of the pan and brush the top of the roll with butter.

7. Bake the strudel until golden brown on all surfaces, 30 to 45 minutes. Let cool on the pan on a wire rack for at least 4 hours before cutting. To serve, sift confectioners' sugar over the top, if desired, and cut crosswise into eight equal slices.

APPLE STRUDEL

APFELSTRUDEL

TALKING ABOUT APPLE STRUDEL with a German is a little like talking to an Italian about the long-cooked pasta sauce that his or her *nonna* makes for Sunday supper: it's familiar, nostalgic, and comforting—and his or her family recipe is the best. This version of strudel is actually one of the most traditional recipes in this book, as it's an extremely popular dessert everyone seems to know. This filling instead relies on a specific blend of ten spices to do the heavy lifting.

INGREDIENTS (SERVES 8)

FILLING

5 lb/2.3 kg Granny Smith apples, peeled, cored, and cut into uneven 1-in/2.5-cm chunks

2¼ tsp Spice Mix (recipe follows)

¾ tsp kosher salt

1½ cups/300 g granulated sugar

½ cup/115 g unsalted butter

¾ tsp vanilla extract

One 1-lb/455-g box phyllo dough, thawed if frozen and at room temperature

1 cup/225 g unsalted butter, melted

Confectioners' sugar for dusting

1. *To make the filling,* preheat the oven to 350°F/180°C.

2. Dump the apples into a large baking dish; sprinkle with the spice mix, salt, and granulated sugar; and toss to coat the apples evenly. Spread the apples in an even layer. Cut the butter into 1-in/2.5-cm pieces and scatter evenly over the apples.

3. Bake the apples, stirring them every 20 minutes, for about 1½ hours. The apples are ready when about half of them are broken down and the other half are still in chunks. Remove from the oven, add the vanilla to the apples, stir to distribute evenly, and then pour the apples onto a sheet pan and let cool to room temperature. Cover and refrigerate until cold, 1 to 2 hours.

4. Preheat the oven to 375°F/190°C. Line a sheet pan with parchment paper.

5. Unroll the stack of phyllo dough on a clean work surface. Remove one sheet from the stack, lay it on the parchment-lined pan, and brush it lightly with melted butter. Continue stacking the sheets on the parchment, brushing each one lightly with butter, until you have 15 layers. Reserve any remaining phyllo sheets for another use. (When you are not removing sheets from the stack, keep the stack covered with plastic wrap to prevent the sheets from drying out.)

(Continued)

6. Position the sheet pan so a long side of the phyllo stack is facing you. Working about 2 in/5 cm from the edge of the dough nearest you, spoon half of the filling in a row along the length of the stack, stopping about 6 in/15 cm short of the both ends. Fold the edge of the phyllo stack nearest you over the filling, covering it completely. Now, spoon the remaining filling in a row next to the edge of the folded dough sheet. Fold the dough over again away from you, covering the second row of filling, then fold in the sides and finish forming the roll. Position the roll, seam-side down, in the center of the pan, then press down gently on the top of the roll to distribute the filling evenly. Brush the top of the roll with butter.

7. Bake the strudel until golden brown on all surfaces, 30 to 45 minutes. Let cool on the pan on a wire rack for at least 4 hours before cutting. To serve, sift confectioners' sugar over the top and cut crosswise into eight equal slices.

SPICE MIX

INGREDIENTS (SERVES 8)

1 cup/125 g ground cinnamon

¼ cup/25 g ground ginger

1 tsp ground allspice

1 tsp ground cloves

2 tsp ground cardamom

2 tsp ground aniseed

2 tsp ground coriander

2 tsp ground mace

1 tsp ground star anise

1 tsp freshly grated nutmeg

Into a small bowl, sift together the cinnamon, ginger, allspice, cloves, cardamom, aniseed, coriander, mace, star anise, and nutmeg. Transfer to a container with an airtight lid and store in a cool cupboard for up to 1 month, or freeze for up to 6 months. Use the mix to flavor other baked goods or sprinkle it on buttered toast, applesauce, oatmeal, yogurt, rice pudding, or custard.

ALMOND-HONEY TART
MANDELTORTE

NUTS, of all varieties and in all forms, are used in many different kinds of German pastry. This nontraditional tart's filling mimics the consistency of a crunchy, sticky pecan pie, without being as cloyingly sweet. It is even amazing made with smoked almonds: the toasty touch nicely counterbalances the sugar content. The shortcrust pastry, known as *Muerberteig*, yields a deliciously rich, crumbly crust.

INGREDIENTS (MAKES ONE 10-IN/25-CM TART)

PASTRY

2½ cups/340 g all-purpose flour plus more for dusting

½ cup/100 g granulated sugar

½ tsp kosher salt

1 cup/225 g unsalted butter, cubed and chilled

4 egg yolks, lightly beaten

FILLING

4 tbsp/55 g unsalted butter

½ cup/170 g honey

¼ cup/55 g firmly packed dark brown sugar

¾ cup/255 g light corn syrup

½ tsp kosher salt

2 cups/220 g slivered almonds

1½ tbsp brandy

1½ tsp vanilla extract

3 eggs, lightly beaten

Lightly sweetened whipped cream for serving (optional)

1. *To make the pastry,* in a food processor, combine the flour, granulated sugar, and salt and process until well mixed, about 30 seconds. Scatter the butter over the flour mixture and pulse until the mixture resembles coarse meal. Add the egg yolks and pulse until the mixture is slightly yellow and larger clumps have formed.

2. Dump the contents of the processor into a medium bowl and begin to squeeze the dough gently in your hands until it forms a ball. Give the dough a few good kneading turns, ensuring that all ingredients are homogenous. Flatten the dough into a disk, wrap in plastic wrap, and refrigerate for at least 30 minutes or up to 1 day.

3. Remove the dough from the refrigerator, unwrap it, and then begin warming it by gently squeezing the edges of the disk. Sprinkle a decent amount of flour onto a work surface and set the disk on the floured surface. Roll out the dough, starting from the center of the disk and rolling outward to the edges, into a round. Rotate the disk a quarter turn after each pass of the pin to ensure an even thickness and that the dough is not sticking. The round should be about 15 in/ 35 cm in diameter and ¼ in/6 mm thick. Lightly flour the top of the round, then carefully roll the pastry around the pin so that you can lift it off of the work surface.

(Continued)

4. Place one edge of the dough over one end of a fluted 10-in/25-cm tart pan with a removable bottom. Unroll the pastry round into the pan, taking care to leave a little slack so that the dough can be pressed into place. Gently press the dough onto the bottom and the sides of the pan, then roll the pin over the rim of the pan to cut away the excess pastry. (You can gather up the excess dough, cut it into shapes, and bake as sugar cookies or reserve it for another use.) Place the tart shell in the freezer.

5. Preheat the oven to 350°F/180°C.

6. *To make the filling,* in a small saucepan, combine the butter, honey, brown sugar, corn syrup, and salt over medium heat and heat, stirring as needed, until the butter melts and all of the ingredients are well mixed. Remove from the heat and pour into a heatproof bowl. Add the almonds, brandy, and vanilla, stir to mix, and let cool for 10 minutes. Stir in the eggs, mixing well.

7. Pour the filling into the prepared tart shell.

8. Bake the tart until the top is dark golden brown and does not jiggle when the pan is shaken, about 30 minutes. Remove from the oven and let cool in the pan on a wire rack for at least 2 hours.

9. Remove the ring from the tart pan and, using an offset spatula, transfer the tart from the pan bottom to a serving plate. Cut the tart into wedges and serve at room temperature with a dollop of whipped cream, if desired. Cover any leftover tart and refrigerate for up to 3 days; bring to room temperature before serving.

HAZELNUT, DARK CHOCOLATE, AND WHITE CHOCOLATE TORTE

HASELNUSSTORTE

THIS IS EVERYONE'S FAVORITE. It's been on our menu for three years, and every time we think it is time to remove it, someone makes a good case to keep it on the list. People often compare it to Nutella or Ferrero Rocher. The cookie-like crust, made from hazelnut flour, supports layers of dark chocolate ganache, hazelnut–white chocolate mousse, and a topping of crushed toasted hazelnuts. Servers at the restaurant sometimes even order this for themselves and eat it after their shifts. That tells you how special it is! This filling is also delicious served in the shortcrust pastry used for the Almond-Honey Tart (page 213).

INGREDIENTS (MAKES ONE 9-IN/23-CM TORTE)

CRUST	GANACHE	MOUSSE AND TOPPING
1½ cups/115 g hazelnut flour	6 oz/170 g dark chocolate, chopped	3½ cups/525 g blanched hazelnuts
⅔ cup/70 g whole-wheat flour	1 cup/240 ml heavy cream	1 lb/455 g white chocolate
½ cup plus 1 tbsp/115 g sugar		2 cups/480 ml heavy cream, whipped to stiff peaks
¾ cup/170 g unsalted butter, melted		

1. *To make the crust,* preheat the oven to 375°F/190°C. In a medium bowl, combine the hazelnut flour, whole-wheat flour, sugar, and butter and stir with a spoon until a soft dough forms. Transfer the dough to a 9-in/23-cm round springform pan and press it onto the bottom in an even layer.

2. Bake the crust until golden, about 15 minutes. Let cool completely on a cooling rack.

3. *To make the ganache,* put the dark chocolate in a heatproof bowl. In a small saucepan, bring the cream to a simmer over medium heat. Remove from the heat, pour the hot cream over the chocolate, and let sit for a couple minutes. With a whisk, stir the cream and chocolate together until the chocolate is completely melted.

4. Pour the ganache onto the cooled crust, spreading it evenly with a rubber spatula. Place the ganache layer in the freezer to set.

(Continued)

5. *To make the mousse and topping,* preheat the oven to 350°F/180°C. Spread all of the hazelnuts on a sheet pan and toast until golden brown, about 20 minutes. Remove from the oven and let cool completely.

6. When the nuts are almost cool, put the white chocolate in a heatproof bowl and place over (not touching) gently simmering water in a saucepan. Heat, stirring occasionally, until the chocolate has melted.

7. Transfer 3 cups/455 g of the nuts to a food processor and process until it becomes a smooth free-flowing butter. This may take a few minutes, and you will need to stop the processor several times to scrape down the sides of the bowl.

8. Remove the melted chocolate from the heat, pour in the hazelnut butter, and stir to combine. Let cool for 20 minutes. Using a rubber spatula, fold the whipped cream, one-third at a time, into the partially cooled chocolate mixture. Pour this mixture evenly over top of the frozen ganache layer.

9. Crush the remaining ½ cup/70 g hazelnuts and sprinkle them evenly over the top of the mousse. Place the torte in the refrigerator for at least 4 hours or preferably overnight. (At this point, the torte can be stored for up to 3 days.)

10. Warm up the sides of the pan by rubbing your hands around the outside. Unclip the sides and lift off the ring. Using an offset spatula, carefully transfer the torte from the pan bottom to a serving plate. Cut into wedges to serve.

BEE STING CAKE
BIENENSTICH

THIS IS ONE OF THE MOST TRADITIONAL DESSERTS IN GERMANY. You'll find it in every bakery in every town in the country. It starts with a yeasted dough covered with an almond caramel mixture that melts into the cake as it bakes. After baking, the cake is sliced in half and filled with a light pastry cream. This recipe has not been updated—it is perfect just as it has always been made.

INGREDIENTS (MAKES ONE 9-IN/23-CM CAKE)

DOUGH

2 tbsp unsalted butter

3½ tbsp/75 g honey

1 cup/240 ml whole milk

Grated zest of 1 lemon

4 cups/560 g all-purpose flour

¾ tsp kosher salt

1 oz/30 g fresh yeast

1 egg

Nonstick cooking spray for preparing the bowl

TOPPING

¼ cup/50 g sugar

6 tbsp/125 g honey

½ cup plus 1 tbsp/130 g unsalted butter

2 cups/220 g slivered almonds

1 tbsp vanilla extract

PASTRY CREAM

2 cups/480 ml whole milk

¼ cup/50 g sugar, plus ⅓ cup/65 g

1 whole egg, plus 2 egg yolks

¼ cup/30 g cornstarch

2 tbsp unsalted butter

1 tsp vanilla extract

¼ tsp kosher salt

1. *To make the dough,* in a small saucepan, combine the butter, honey, and milk over low heat and heat until the butter melts and the mixture is blended. Set aside to cool for about 10 minutes, then stir in the lemon zest. Meanwhile, in a medium bowl, stir together the flour and salt.

2. Crumble the yeast into the cooled milk mixture, stir to dissolve, and then whisk in the egg until blended. Pour this mixture into the bowl of a stand mixer and slowly stir in the flour until a soft dough forms.

3. Fit the mixer with the dough hook and knead on low speed until the dough is smooth and the flour is completely saturated, about 2 minutes.

4. Coat a large, clean bowl with cooking spray, transfer the dough to the bowl, cover the bowl with plastic wrap, and set aside in a warm spot until the dough doubles in volume, about 45 minutes.

(Continued)

5. When the dough is ready, press it into the bottom of a 9-in/23-cm round springform pan, forming an even layer. Set aside.

6. Preheat the oven to 350°F/180°C.

7. *To make the topping,* in a small, heavy saucepan, combine the sugar, honey, butter, and almonds over high heat and bring to a boil, stirring occasionally to dissolve the sugar. Let the mixture boil until it begins to turn lightly golden, 7 to 10 minutes. Remove from the heat and stir in the vanilla.

8. Pour the topping over the dough and spread it an even layer with a heatproof spatula. Bake until the top is golden brown and a cake tester or toothpick inserted into the center comes out dry, about 20 minutes. Let the cake cool in the pan on a wire rack.

9. *To make the pastry cream,* in a small, heavy saucepan, combine the milk and ¼ cup/50 g sugar and bring to a boil over medium-high heat, stirring occasionally to dissolve the sugar. Meanwhile, in a bowl, whisk together the whole egg, egg yolks, cornstarch, and remaining ⅓ cup/ 65 g sugar until blended.

10. When the milk reaches a boil, immediately remove it from the heat and slowly pour half of it into the egg mixture while whisking constantly. Then pour the contents of the bowl back into the pan while whisking constantly. Return the pan to medium heat and heat, whisking constantly. When you see the first few bubbles break on the surface of the custard, immediately remove the pan from the heat and pour the custard into a clean bowl. Stir in the butter, vanilla, and salt until the butter melts, then cover with plastic wrap, pressing it directly onto the surface of the custard to prevent a skin from forming. Let cool until lukewarm, then refrigerate until cold, about 2 hours.

11. Unclip the sides of the springform pan and lift off the ring. Using an offset spatula, transfer the cake from the pan bottom to a serving plate. Using a long, serrated knife, cut the cake in half horizontally, creating two even layers. Remove the top layer and spread the pastry cream evenly onto the bottom layer. Replace the top layer.

12. Cut the cake into wedges to serve, or cover and refrigerate until serving. It will keep refrigerated for up to 5 days.

QUARK CHEESECAKE WITH PRETZEL CRUST

TOPFENTORTE

THE FILLING FOR THIS CHEESECAKE IS nothing like the thick, intensely rich New York–style cake. Made with quark and lightened with egg whites, this cake is more like a sweet cheese soufflé than a cheesecake. The crust, which is made with crushed hard pretzels, also helps to set this cake apart.

INGREDIENTS (MAKES ONE 10-IN/25-CM TART)

CRUST

1½ cups/345 g finely ground hard pretzels

¼ cup/50 g sugar

½ cup/115 g unsalted butter, melted

FILLING

8 oz/225 g cream cheese, at room temperature

1 lb/455 g quark or farmer cheese

1¼ cups/250 g sugar

3 eggs, separated

1 tsp vanilla extract

1. *To make the crust,* preheat the oven to 375°F/190°C. In a bowl, combine the ground pretzels, sugar, and butter and stir until well mixed and evenly moistened. Transfer the mixture to a 10-in/25-cm springform pan with a removable bottom and press it onto the bottom in an even layer.

2. Bake the crust until golden, about 15 minutes. Remove from the oven and let cool completely on a cooling rack. Lower the oven temperature to 300°F/150°C.

3. *To make the filling,* in a food processor, combine both cheeses, 1 cup/200 g of the sugar, the egg yolks, and vanilla and process until completely smooth, 5 to 7 minutes. Transfer to a large bowl.

4. In a stand mixer fitted with the whisk attachment, beat the egg whites on medium-high speed until foamy. Slowly pour the remaining ¼ cup/50 g sugar into the egg whites and beat on medium-high speed until soft peaks form.

5. Using a rubber spatula, fold the beaten whites, one-third at a time, into the cheese mixture. Pour the batter into the prepared crust.

6. Bake the cheesecake until the edges are golden and the center does not jiggle when the pan is shaken, 30 to 45 minutes. Let cool in the pan on a wire rack to room temperature.

7. Unclip the sides and lift off the ring. Using an offset spatula, carefully transfer the cheesecake from the pan bottom to a serving plate. Cut into wedges to serve. It will keep, covered with plastic wrap, at room temperature for up to 5 days.

MALTED POTS DE CRÈME
MALZKREME

THIS IS THE IDEAL RECIPE to have on hand if company is coming and you are stuck on what to make for dessert. It's just so easy: honey-sweetened cream is mixed with malted milk powder and a little gelatin and then poured into ramekins and left to set in the refrigerator. It can be served plain or topped with a medley of fresh berries, with a raspberry sauce, or even with chocolate-dipped pretzel sticks.

INGREDIENTS (SERVES 4)

2 cups/480 ml heavy cream	½ vanilla bean	2 tbsp plus 2 tsp honey
1½ tsp powdered gelatin	¾ cup/105 g malted milk powder	½ tsp kosher salt

1. Put ¼ cup/60 ml of the cream in a small bowl, stir in the gelatin, and set aside. Pour the remaining 1¾ cups/420 ml cream into a saucepan. Split the vanilla bean in half lengthwise. Using the tip of the knife, scrape the seeds from the halves into the pan, then toss in the pod halves. Place the pan over medium heat and heat until small bubbles appear around the edges of the pan. Immediately remove from the heat and set aside for 1 hour.

2. Return the pan to medium heat. When the cream begins to steam, whisk in the milk powder, honey, and salt until well mixed. Add the bloomed gelatin and whisk just until melted; do not allow the mixture to boil. Immediately remove the pan from the heat and pour the custard through a fine-mesh sieve placed over a heatproof pitcher large enough to hold the custard.

3. Pour the custard into four ½-cup/120-ml ramekins, dividing it evenly. Cover the ramekins, transfer to the refrigerator, and chill until the custard is set, at least 4 hours. (The pots de crème will keep for up to 5 days.)

4. Pour very hot water into a shallow bowl; the water should be about half the depth of a ramekin. One at a time, place the ramekins in the bowl just long enough to loosen the sides of the custard, then invert an individual serving plate on top of the ramekin and invert the ramekin and serving plate together, releasing the custard onto the plate. It should come out easily, if not, run a thin knife blade around the edge of the custard to loosen it. Serve immediately.

STEAMED PLUM-STUFFED SWEET YEASTED DUMPLINGS

DAMPFNUDELN MIT PFLAUMEN

THERE'S NOTHING FANCY or expensive about these sweet little plum-stuffed dumplings. They're steamed in a pan on the stove top, which is a bit tricky to do, but if done correctly, results in a beautiful caramelized bottom crust. We drizzle the finished dumplings with a vanilla sauce flavored with anise, ginger, clove, and allspice.

INGREDIENTS (SERVES 8)

1½ tsp active dry yeast

4 tbsp sugar

¼ cup/60 ml warm water

¾ cup/180 ml whole milk, warmed, plus ½ cup/120 ml

2 tbsp unsalted butter, melted, plus 2 tbsp

¼ tsp salt

2 cups/280 g all-purpose flour, sifted, plus more for dusting

Nonstick cooking spray for preparing the pan

2 black plums

1 tbsp cornstarch

¼ tsp ground cardamom

Spiced Vanilla Sauce (recipe follows)

1. In a small bowl, dissolve the yeast and 1 tbsp of the sugar in the warm water. Let stand until foamy, about 5 minutes.

2. In a medium bowl, stir together the warmed milk, melted butter, 1 tbsp sugar, the salt, and the yeast mixture. Add the flour and stir with a spoon until a soft dough forms.

3. Lightly flour a work surface and turn the dough out onto it. Knead until firm but moist, about 5 minutes.

4. Coat a sheet pan with nonstick cooking spray. Divide the dough into eight equal portions, roll each portion into a ball, and place on the prepared sheet pan, spacing them evenly apart. Cover the pan loosely with plastic wrap and place in a warm spot until the balls double in size, about 45 minutes.

5. Cut each plum lengthwise into quarters and discard the pits. In a small bowl, toss the plums with the cornstarch and cardamom, coating evenly. Set aside.

6. When the dough balls have risen, uncover them. Pick up a ball, flatten it about halfway, top with a plum quarter, and them wrap the dough around the plum, reshaping the dough into a ball. Pinch the edges together tightly to seal and return the ball to the sheet pan. Repeat with the remaining dough balls and plum quarters. Re-cover the sheet pan with plastic wrap and return it to the warm spot. Let the dough rise for 10 minutes.

7. Preheat a 10-in/25-cm frying pan over medium heat. Add the 2 tbsp butter, and when it has melted, add the ½ cup/120 ml milk and the remaining 2 tbsp sugar and bring the mixture to a boil. Add the dumplings to the pan, arranging them close together so they will all fit, and cover the pan with a tight-fitting lid. Turn the heat to low and cook, undisturbed, for 15 minutes. Uncover the pan and check to see if the dumplings are ready. They are done if the liquid has disappeared and the bottom of the pan is covered with a golden crust.

8. To unmold, gently sweep a spatula around the perimeter of the dumplings to loosen them, then turn them out onto a plate. If some of them are stuck to the pan bottom, use the spatula to free them gently from the pan. Serve immediately.

SPICED VANILLA SAUCE
VANILLESAUCE MIT GEWÜRZEN

INGREDIENTS (MAKES 2½ CUPS/600 ML)

2 cups/475 ml heavy cream	6 egg yolks	½ tsp kosher salt
2 tbsp Spice Mix (page 212)	½ cup/115 g sugar	¾ tsp vanilla extract
½ vanilla bean		

1. Put a medium bowl into the fridge to chill.

2. Pour the heavy cream into a small saucepan. With the tip of a knife, split the vanilla bean lengthwise and scrape out the seeds. Add the vanilla seeds and pod to the cream and place over medium heat. Bring the cream to a simmer, then remove from the heat and let steep for 30 minutes.

3. In a small bowl, whisk the Spice Mix, egg yolks, sugar, and salt together until combined.

4. Return the cream to medium-low heat. When it begins to steam, slowly pour half of the cream over the yolk mixture, whisking constantly. Pour the cream-yolk mixture slowly back into the pan with the remaining cream. Cook, stirring constantly with a rubber spatula, until the mixture thickens enough to coat the back of a spoon. Remove from the heat and immediately pour through a sieve placed over the chilled bowl. (Reserve the vanilla bean and add it back to the sauce to continue flavoring it.) Stir in the vanilla extract.

5. Let cool slightly, stirring occasionally, and then pour into an airtight container and transfer to the refrigerator to chill completely before using, at least 2 hours. Remove the vanilla bean before using. The sauce will keep for up to 5 days.

ROASTED APRICOTS WITH SPICED DARK LAGER SAUCE

APRIKOSENKOMPOTT

THIS HEADY SAUCE, with its dark lager base, ripe apricots, and warm spices, is a great topping for ice cream or pound cake. Its dark, malty stone-fruit flavors also mean that whatever dessert it tops will pair well with a comparably constructed beer.

INGREDIENTS (MAKES 2 QT/2 G)

¾ cup/115 g dark raisins

1 cup/225 g firmly packed dark brown sugar

2 cups/480 ml dark lager, preferably Warsteiner Premium Dunkel

1 cinnamon stick

1 star anise pod

5 thin coins of sliced fresh ginger

1 tsp kosher salt

2 tbsp all-purpose flour

1 vanilla bean

2 lb/910 g apricots, halved and pitted

1. Preheat the oven to 375°F/190°C.

2. In a medium bowl, whisk together the raisins, brown sugar, lager, cinnamon stick, star anise pod, ginger, salt, and flour. Split the vanilla bean in half lengthwise, then, using the tip of the knife, scrape the seeds from the halves into the bowl and whisk to combine.

3. Put the apricots into a baking dish just large enough to accommodate them (they do not need to be in a single layer). Pour the raisin mixture evenly overly the apricots.

4. Roast, uncovered, until the apricots begin to split and soften, about 45 minutes. Remove from the oven, transfer to a heatproof dish, and let cool to room temperature.

5. Use immediately, or pack into one or more jars or other airtight containers and store in the refrigerator for up to 1 month.

ACKNOWLEDGMENTS

I don't even know where to start. There are so many people in my life who have helped shape my career—and this book—in ways unimaginable!

Jessica, I can't thank you enough for always being there for me and for embracing what it means to be married to a chef. You've been a great wife, friend, listener, and mother to the kids while I've worked, traveled, and scrambled to get this book done. I love you so much and look forward to everything life brings us.

Aidan and Kiera, even though only one of you can read this right now, I'm hoping this book will be an inspiration to you and show you that with hard work and persistence you can make just about anything happen. Life wouldn't be complete without my little buddy and my princess. I love you guys more than anything.

Mom and Dad, everything you've done for me has shaped what I am today. Mom, you've always been so supportive of me no matter what I've done, and you've shown me how to be a better person. Thanks for always being there to listen to whatever I was going through. Dad, you've taught me so much over the years, from giving me my first guitar and showing me how to play to bringing me into the restaurants where you were the chef and getting me started in the kitchen. Even though you told me repeatedly that I shouldn't become a chef, I ended up in the business anyway. I guess the joke's on you! I love you guys and am grateful for everything you've done for me.

Doug and Kelly, I probably wouldn't have written this book if you hadn't dreamed of opening a German restaurant in Philly. It's been a great ride so far and I look forward to many more amazing years at Brauhaus, Wursthaus, and all of our future

endeavors. Thanks for everything you do, and for allowing me to take Zigeunerschnitzel off the menu.

Thanks to everyone at Brauhaus Schmitz for all of your hard work and dedication. It's been a great five years and it's only going to get better. I'd like to acknowledge the handful of you who have been with us since the beginning and who continue to do an amazing job! Thank you, Brett, Brian, Alex, Amelia, Brendan, Hugo, Azul, Beate, and Ray.

Henrik Ringbom, it's been great working with you over the years. We've had a lot of fun and have done some amazing things! Thanks for running the kitchen while I'm traveling or working on the book or opening new places. You're the man, Hammer.

Clare Pelino, I appreciate all that you did to make this book a reality. When you approached me years ago about writing a book, I didn't think it could ever happen, but your persistence and hard work got it done. I look forward to working with you again and writing more books in the future.

Drew Lazor, thanks for hanging out with me and listening to me talk about the recipes and the inspirations, and for not looking at me as if I was speaking, well, German! It's been a lot of fun, and it's so rewarding to see it all come together.

Jason Varney, thanks for having such a great photographic vision. Without you and Carrie, the photos would never have looked so amazing, and the book so awesome.

Thanks to the whole crew at Chronicle Books who worked so hard on this project. A big thank-you to my editor Sarah Billingsley for listening to all my questions and for making this book special.

RESOURCES

Border Springs Farm
Lamb
www.borderspringsfarm.com

Butcher & Packer
Sausage-making equipment and ingredients
www.butcher-packer.com

The Chefs' Warehouse
Specialty foods and ingredients
www.chefswarehouse.com

D'Artagnan
Gourmet foods, including foie gras, quail, and truffles
www.dartagnan.com

Di Bruno Bros.
Imported and domestic cheeses and cured meats
www.dibruno.com

Fante's
Cooking equipment, including springerle molds
www.fantes.com

German Deli
German and Scandinavian ingredients
www.germandeli.com

Home Sweet Homebrew
Malt powder, smoked barley malt, air locks for sauerkraut
www.homesweethomebrew.com

Hudson Valley Foie Gras
Foie gras and foie gras products
www.hudsonvalleyfoiegras.com

Northern Brewer
Malt powder, smoked barley malt, air locks for sauerkraut
www.northernbrewer.com

Philly Homebrew Outlet
Malt powder, smoked barley malt, air locks for sauerkraut
www.phillyhomebrew.com

Previn
Specialty cookware and baking supplies
www.previninc.com

Rieker's Prime Meats
Sausages, headcheese, cheeses, and foods imported from Germany
www.riekersmeats.com

The Sausage Maker
Sausage-making equipment and ingredients
www.sausagemaker.com

A Soapy Sailor
Lye for pretzels
www.asoapysailor.com

Wursthaus Schmitz
Sausages and foods imported from Germany
www.brauhausschmitz.com

INDEX